"I AM JOE'S BODY"
"I AM JANE'S BODY"

Beginning with the publication of "I AM JOE'S HEART" in 1967, J. D. Ratcliff's fascinating articles about the human body quickly established themselves as the most successful series ever run in *Reader's Digest*. Over the years, the magazine answered requests with over seven million reprints of individual articles!

"I AM JOE'S BODY"

●   ●   ●   ●   ●   ●

READER'S DIGEST PAPERBACKS

Informative .... *Entertaining* .... *Essential* ....

Berkley, one of America's leading paperback publishers, is proud to present this special series of the best-loved articles, stories and features from America's most trusted magazine. Each is a one-volume library on a popular and important subject. And each is selected, edited and endorsed by the Editors of *Reader's Digest* themselves! Watch for these others...

THE ART OF LIVING
SECRETS OF THE PAST
TESTS AND TEASERS

"I AM JOE'S BODY"

BY J.D. RATCLIFF

FOREWORD BY HOWARD A. RUSK, M.D.
ILLUSTRATIONS BY ROBERT J. DEMAREST

A BERKLEY/READER'S DIGEST BOOK
published by
BERKLEY BOOKS, NEW YORK

This Berkley book contains the complete
text of the original hardcover edition.
It has been completely reset in a type face
designed for easy reading, and was printed
from new film.

"I AM JOE'S BODY"
originally published as YOUR BODY & HOW IT
WORKS

A Berkley Book / published by arrangement with
Reader's Digest Press

PRINTING HISTORY
Reader's Digest Press and Delacorte Press edition
published 1975
Berkley / Reader's Digest Edition / April 1980
Fourth printing / April 1981

Cover design by Sam Salant.

ISBN: 0-425-04550-1

A BERKLEY BOOK® TM 757,375
Berkley Books are published by Berkley Publishing
Corporation,
200 Madison Avenue, New York, New York 10016.
PRINTED IN THE UNITED STATES OF AMERICA

For Margaret

ACKNOWLEDG-MENTS

Grateful acknowledgment is made to the following distinguished physicians, surgeons and research men who assisted with interviews in preparation of this book: Drs. Henry F. Allen, Harvey Blank, Lewis E. Braverman, Algie C. Brown, William W. Cleveland, William D. Davis, Jr., Richard G. Eaton, Daniel S. Ellis, Humberto Fernández-Morán, Lawrence M. Fishman, Irving Glickman, Francisco Gonzales, Hurst B. Hatch, Robert I. Henkin, Howard P. House, John K. Lattimer, William J. LeMaire, Choh Hao Li, Dale Lindholm, J. William Littler, John M. Marsh, Daniel Mintz, Alton Ochsner, Irvine H. Page, Kenneth Savard, Edward B. Schlesinger, Albert Segaloff, Arthur G. Shapiro, Landrum B. Shettles, David A. Spring, Frank E. Stinchfield, Harold G. Tabb, Donald Tapley, Leon Walker, Jack Wickstrom, Alexander S. Wiener, Philip D. Wilson, Jr., Irving S. Wright.

The author is particularly indebted to DeWitt Wallace, Hobart Lewis and James McCracken of *Reader's Digest*, in which magazine this material appeared in slightly different form.

CONTENTS

JOE AND JANE

Joe is a typical American man. His wife, Jane, is a typical American woman. Joe is 47, Jane is 42, and they have three children.

Their organs (some are exclusively Joe's, some are Jane's, but most are common to both sexes) have told their stories in a series of articles that first appeared in *Reader's Digest*. Those articles, the most popular series in the magazine's history, form the basis of this book.

FOREWORD

To write the facts of science for the general reader, and to make them interesting, palatable and exciting, is a work of art. It requires a special, sensitive sixth sense of understanding, like that of a musician who has perfect tone perception. One note below or above means discord. The same true sensitive perception is fundamental in science writing. If the tone of the writing is just one note too low, some readers will say, "He's writing down to me. I'm not a child." If the tone is even a single note too high, the reader will comment, "This is highbrow stuff. I don't understand it. I'm not interested." Perfect balance and perfect pitch are necessary if science writing is to be fact and not fiction.

J. D. Ratcliff's writing displays these great gifts. He is capable of translating hard scientific facts into bright, scintillating, exciting and unforgettable knowledge. He presents Joe and Jane as a gracious, friendly couple who introduce the organs and tissues of their bodies, sharing their secrets with the reader. The result of this guided tour is a scientific documentary that reads like a novel.

But Joe and Jane's story is not fiction; the facts have been analyzed, not only by the author but by hosts of distinguished scientists who have put their stamp of approval on the authenticity of these facts. This book provides the reader with a basic understanding of the sensitive and unbelievably complex way in which all the members of his body's team function to make him the person he is.

Rarely can one read for pleasure and emerge with fundamental, lasting knowledge. This is especially true when it involves one's own body. This book should be invaluable to students. It is important not only for those in the health and science field, but should provide core health knowledge for all students—young and old. It even provides a valuable review course for professionals in the health field who have forgotten some of the facts they learned many years ago, or missed some of the new knowledge that has evolved from the thousands of research laboratories manned by tens of thousands of scientists throughout the world.

The author has provided us with a new understanding, not just of our own bodies and minds but of life itself. The reader cannot turn the pages of this book without feeling wiser, richer and happier, because he will appreciate more deeply his very own life, and what makes it possible.

HOWARD A. RUSK, M.D.

"I AM JOE'S BODY"

1
The Basic
Unit

CELL

I AM SOMETHING LIKE a big city. I have dozens of power stations, a transportation system, a sophisticated communications setup. I import raw materials, manufacture goods, operate a garbage-disposal system. I have an efficient government—a rigid dictatorship, really—and I police my precincts to keep out undesirables.

All this in something *my* size? It takes a good microscope to even *see* me, and a supermicroscope to peep inside my metropolis! I am a cell, one of the 60 *trillion* in Joe's body. The cell is often called the basic element of life. Actually, we're life itself. As a rod cell in Joe's right eye, I will speak for the vast population of which I am a member.

There is no such thing as a "typical" cell. We are as different in form and function as a giraffe and a mouse. We come in all sizes, the largest of all being an ostrich egg. From there we scale down to a point where a million of us could sit comfortably on the head of a pin. And we come in a variety of shapes—discs, rods, spheres.

We participate in everything Joe does. He lifts a suitcase and

3

The Basic Unit

thinks his arm is doing the job. Actually, it's invisible muscle cells, contracting. Let him ponder which necktie to wear: it's brain cells that do the pondering. Or he shaves his face: nerve and muscle cells perform the entire operation. For that matter, the facial hairs he chops off were produced by other cells.

My task as a rod cell in the eye is to catch faint light—say the twinkle of a star—simplify it and change it into an electrical signal, which I then send to Joe's brain. If enough signals arrive, he "sees" the star.

Since each of us 250 million rod cells in Joe's eyes contains 30 million molecules of light-catching pigment, we naturally use a lot of electricity. To generate it, I have some thousand mitochondria—superminute, sausage-shaped power stations that burn fuel (sugar), produce electricity and leave "ash" (water and carbon dioxide) behind. In this complex chemical process they synthesize a substance called adenosine triphosphate—ATP for short. It is the universal power source for every living thing, from rhubarb to clams to man.

When there is need for energy—to make the heart beat, to expand the chest in breathing, to blink an eyelid—ATP breaks down into simpler substances, releasing power as it does. As long as Joe lives, there will be this call for energy and ATP. Even in deepest sleep there is a torrent of activity—cellular furnaces burning to keep the body warm, brain cells discharging electricity to make dreams, heart cells pulsing to keep blood flowing. The breakdown (and building up) of ATP is constant.

All of us cells have mitochondria, with one notable exception: red blood cells. Since they do no manufacturing and are swept along by the bloodstream, they have no need for power.

Perhaps the ultimate wonder among cells is the female egg, as in the body of Joe's mother. Once fertilized, this single cell divides over and over, until there are the two trillion cells of a baby. Phenomenal as such multiplication is in itself, the truly striking thing is the enormous amount of information stored within the fertilized egg. That tiny fragment of life contains the blueprint for building that complex chemical plant, the liver. It stores coded information on hair color, skin texture, body size. It knows just when to shut off growth of a little finger. Even at

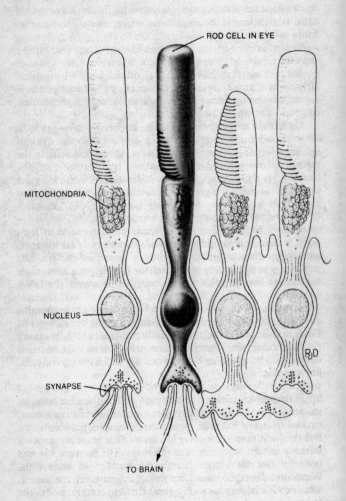

ROD CELL IN EYE

MITOCHONDRIA

NUCLEUS

SYNAPSE

TO BRAIN

the outset, it knows approximately how bright Joe may be years later, what diseases he might be susceptible to, his general appearance.

How does one tiny egg (they are all about the same size in the mammalian world) know to make a whale, another a rabbit, another a Joe? This gets us to that miracle stuff of creation, DNA—deoxyribonucleic acid. The dictator of all us cells, it tells our cellular components how to behave, what to manufacture, what to seek, what to avoid.

My DNA can be compared to an architect whose job is to draw up the grand design for living. But it hands the work of building over to contractors—RNA, or ribonucleic acid. In the form of molecules, all information is "printed" on the interlocking twin spirals of DNA. "Messenger" RNA snuggles up to DNA spirals and gets a blueprint of what is wanted. It then passes the word along to another form of RNA, "transfer" RNA. And the latter starts to work according to instructions— most likely building one of the hundreds of proteins in Joe's body. It takes the 20-odd amino acids that proteins are made of, and strings them together like beads in a specified pattern. The result may be a pulsating muscle cell for Joe's heart, a contractile leg muscle that permits him to walk, or whatever the DNA ordered.

Surprisingly, the DNA in the rod cells of Joe's eyes contains all the information needed to produce a complete baby! The DNA in an ear cell could theoretically construct a foot. We don't do these nonsensical things because in each of us large portions of the DNA template are blocked out. My DNA makes rod cells, nothing else.

The cellular division that created Joe continues throughout life. Each second, millions of cells die—and millions are born, by the process of old cells pulling apart, each to make two new ones, exact duplicates. Fat cells, large storage bins, reproduce slowly. But skin cells reproduce every ten hours. One notable exception to this constant replacement is the brain. The moment Joe was born he had his lifetime maximum number of brain cells. Worn-out, damaged ones keep dying; they are never replaced. Yet Joe's initial surplus was so great that he scarcely notices the loss.

We cells manufacture upward of 600 enzymes—most remarkable substances. On orders from RNA, these master chemists instantly and effortlessly synthesize proteins—taking protein from a piece of fish, breaking it down into its components and rearranging the amino acids to make the human proteins needed for, say, Joe's thumbnail. Cellular enzymes also build bafflingly complex hormones and disease-fighting antibodies, and perform many tasks beyond the capabilities of the world's most gifted chemists.

Just as remarkable as our internal structure is our external wall. My membrane is a bare .0000001 millimeter thick. Until very recently, scientists thought of this gossamer covering as little more than a kind of tight cellophane bag. Thanks to the electron microscope, they now realize that it is one of my most important components. Acting as gatekeeper, the cellular membrane decides what shall be admitted, what excluded. It controls the cell's internal environment—keeping in exact balance salts, organic materials, water and other substances. Life is absolutely dependent on this.

Which raw materials are wanted for protein manufacture? The membrane admits the right one, excludes others. Obviously it has a sophisticated recognition system.

Each of us carries an identification tag, recognized by other cell membranes. Any foreigner or intruder is simply chased away from our individual colonies. Imagine what would happen if we tolerated strangers. A hair cell might wander into my area, and hair would soon sprout from Joe's eyes. Warts might start growing in his kidneys, liver cells on his eyelids.

The membrane also seems to have a communications system to talk to other cells. How it functions I don't know—enzymes again, maybe? Anyway, if you take a heart apart, separating it into individual cells, those cells will pulse at random. But soon they will be beating in unison again! Somehow the word gets around.

Hormones are also part of the communications system, acting as chemical messengers. For example: Joe's blood sugar starts rising. His pancreas steps up production of insulin, the hormone that says, "Speed up burning of sugar." The bloodstream carries this work order around and the cells respond. Or, Joe may decide to chop some wood. He will need extra energy. In this case his thyroid sends the hormonal work order to cells: "Speed up production of ATP."

Our great enemies are the viruses. These pesky little parasites have no mitochondria—they are unable to produce their own power for living. From time to time, our membrane guardians fall down on the job and a virus penetrates a cell. With power now available, these terrors start reproducing. Overwhelmed by virus particles, the unfortunate cell perishes. Then the released virus attacks other cells. In even the mildest virus infections, millions of cells perish. If it were not for a variety of body defenses, the viruses would take over, and Joe wouldn't be long for this world.

Perhaps the story of cells can best be summed up by saying that we are where it all takes place—everything from Joe's beginning to his end. How 60 trillion of us can live in such harmony—each minding his own business, efficiently performing his own tasks—is something to contemplate. It is a wonder. Maybe it is the supreme wonder.

2

Central Nervous System

BRAIN

COMPARED TO ME, other wonders of the universe pale into insignificance. I am a three-pound mushroom of gray and white tissue of gelatinous consistency. No computer exists that can duplicate all my myriad functions. My component parts are staggering in number: some 30 billion neurons and five to ten times that number of glial cells. And all this fitted into the crown of a size 7 hat! I am Joe's brain.

But I'm not just part of Joe, I *am* Joe—his personality, his reactions, his mental capacity. He thinks that he hears with his ears, tastes with his tongue, feels with his fingers. All these things happen inside of me—ears, tongue and fingers merely gather information. I tell him when he is sick, when he is hungry; I govern his sex urge, his moods, everything.

Even when he is asleep I continue to handle traffic that would swamp all the world's telephone exchanges. The amount of information flooding in on Joe from the outside is staggering. How can I cope with it all? I simply select what is important, and Joe ignores the rest. If Joe puts a phonograph record on and attempts to read at the same time, he will concentrate on the record or the book, but not both. If Joe becomes involved in a particularly good novel, he shouldn't be surprised if he doesn't remember hearing his favorite musical passage.

Of course, if something potentially dangerous happens, I instantly shift gears. Let Joe slip on the ice and I immediately direct him to regain his balance, and then signal his arms to break the fall. Finally, if he hits the ground, I let Joe know if he is hurt. And the event is stored in my memory to warn Joe to walk carefully on ice in the future.

In addition to taking care of such emergencies, I have thousands of housekeeping chores to perform. Overseeing breathing, for example. Sensors inform me that carbon dioxide is rising in Joe's blood and that he needs more oxygen. I step up the breathing rate—timing the contraction and relaxation of chest muscles.

In thousands of such ways I baby Joe. In return, I am piggishly demanding. Although I represent only two percent of Joe's body weight, I require 20 percent of the oxygen he inhales and a fifth of the blood his heart pumps. I am utterly dependent on a constant supply. Let there be a temporary shortage and Joe faints. Let the supply be cut off for a few minutes and I suffer grave damage—paralysis or death may result. I also demand a steady supply of nourishment—glucose. Even in situations of acute starvation, I get first call on any available, for without me Joe would die.

In many respects, I am like a vast, unexplored continent, with little more known than the rough outlines of the shore. But the researchers who are attempting to map me have come up with some fascinating information. For example, although all pain is felt *in* me, I myself have no pain sensation even when I'm cut. Thus, brain surgery is performed with the patient wide awake, allowing the brain explorers to stimulate specific areas of me electrically and observe the response. If Joe ever undergoes such surgery, he will be amazed at what can happen. A tickle of electricity in one place and he might "see" a long-forgotten third-grade teacher. Stimulated in other places, he might "hear" a train whistle or a recitation of a nursery rhyme he couldn't have recalled a few hours earlier. I'm like an old attic containing mementos of a lifetime. Joe might not be aware of what it is in the attic, but it's there.

The brain mappers have at least a rough outline of my primary functioning areas: vision in the rear, hearing on the sides. Perhaps the most interesting discovery is the "pleasure center." Teach a rat to press a switch that gives a minute electrical prod to the "pleasure center" and the animal will press the switch almost continuously—preferring the stimulation even to food. Given time, it could die of starvation—presumably happily. If Joe ever suffers a severe depression, doctors might implant such an electrode in his brain. Little jolts of electricity could transform a depressed Joe into an ecstatic Joe.

I reside, of course, in a well-protected fortress. The skull is a quarter of an inch thick at the top, and even thicker at the base. I am bathed in a watery fluid that cushions me from shocks. A blood-brain barrier serves as a gatekeeper, letting some things in, denying entrance to others. Thus, it welcomes the glucose I need, but blocks out bacteria and toxic substances. Most painkillers and anesthetics pass in with ease—but so, unfortunately, do alcohol and hallucinogenic drugs that wildly distort my normal activities. I may even "hear" a visual image.

A word about my architecture. Lift a piece of sod from a lawn and note the baffling intertwining of roots. I am something like that—multiplied by millions. Each of my 30 billion nerve cells, or neurons, connects with others—some as many as 60,000 times!

A neuron looks something like a spider attached to a filament. The spider is the cell body, the filament the axon, the legs the dendrites. The legs pick up a signal from adjacent neurons, pass it to the body; the signal is in turn passed along by the filament at speeds up to 225 m.p.h. After each signal passes, it takes the filament about 1/2000 of a second to recharge itself chemically. At no point does one of my neurons touch another; signals are passed spark-gap fashion. At each "firing" one nerve chemically communicates with another.

For all my versatility, I unfortunately never learned the wonders of reproduction. Skin, liver tissue, blood cells can be replaced after damage or loss. But if I lose one of my cells it is lost forever—and by age 35, Joe was losing over 1000 of my nerve cells a day! With age, I also lose weight. But for my great reserves, these things might be disastrous. But I compensate. Let a thousand cells die and a thousand others may never notice the

Central Nervous System

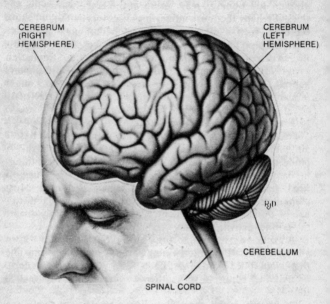

CEREBRUM
(RIGHT
HEMISPHERE)

CEREBRUM
(LEFT
HEMISPHERE)

CEREBELLUM

SPINAL CORD

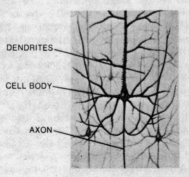

DENDRITES

CELL BODY

AXON

loss. But, if enough cells are destroyed, Joe may. His sense of smell might diminish. His taste could become less acute and hearing fade. Joe might notice his attention span diminishing, and he might have more difficulty remembering names, dates, telephone numbers. But I will take care of the really important jobs to the end.

Joe knows he has two kidneys, two lungs, two adrenals. He doesn't think of me as a "paired" organ, but in a sense I am, in that I have distinct right and left hemispheres. My left half controls much of the activity on the right side of his body, my other hemisphere the left. With right-handed people, the left hemisphere is dominant. With lefties, the reverse is true. Recent studies suggest that my left hemisphere controls Joe's ability to walk, write and do mathematics. My right hemisphere is essentially mute but can do other things, such as make spatial judgments.

Certainly, though, my most striking feature is my backup system. I store each memory in various places—either the sight of an apple tree or the sound of a brook could trigger the same memory of a special spot in Vermont. Thus, it is possible for Joe to manage quite nicely even with part of me destroyed. My remaining part may require considerable time to take over jobs strange to it. But frequently I am able to set up compensating networks of nerve connections. Speech may return, life may come back to paralyzed limbs, cobwebs clear.

This striking adaptability is a lucky thing, for despite my elaborate protections, I am prey to an array of trouble. Tumors can cause a variety of disasters; fortunately, tumor removal, when it is possible, is now almost completely safe and often results in dramatic recoveries.

Stroke is another major problem. A clot forms in one of my small blood vessels or one of my small arteries weakens and bursts, and part of me starves. Symptoms range from minor mental lapses to total paralysis and death. Little can be done to correct the effects of stroke in some cases. In others, rehabilitation is possible. Its success will depend on which part and how much of me has been destroyed.

A third enemy is brain injury. Despite my watery cushion and fortress skull, I can still be slammed around by blows, accidents, falls. I respond in many different ways. I may swell, just as a mashed finger does. But because I am confined in a bony prison, I have no room to swell. Pressure develops. Symptoms range from blackouts to death.

But my comeback powers, as we've seen, are mighty. And my story is by no means over. If my accomplishments to date loom large—speech, memory, reasoning and all the other wonders— they may be as nothing compared to what lies ahead. My resources have barely been tapped. My potential is enormous. For men a few hundred thousand years in the future, I may seem quite as primitive as Neanderthal man's brain seems today.

HYPOTHALAMUS

JOE NEVER HEARD of me. But I am the single most important group of cells in his body—on duty 24 hours a day even though most of the time Joe is not aware of what I am doing. My chief responsibility is maintaining equilibrium inside Joe. I inform other regions of the brain and body that their services are required. As a result of my constant monitoring, Joe knows when he is hungry, thirsty, hot or cold, and how to react to anger or fear. In one way or another, I take part in just about everything he does. I am Joe's hypothalamus, and this is my story.

I'm not bright like other parts of Joe's brain. Thinking is not my business. I suppose you could call me the central switchboard of Joe's body, a sort of coordinator for much of Joe's nervous system and for his pituitary gland (often called the master gland because of its influence on metabolism, growth and secondary sex characteristics, as well as other functions of the hormone system).

I'm quite unimpressive in appearance. I lie near the underside of the brain, just about in the center of Joe's head. I'm pink and gray in color, and approximately the size of a small prune—a mere 1/300 of the mass of the brain. Yet I have a richer blood supply than any other portion of the body, a highly developed sensing system, and extensive direct and indirect nerve connections within the nervous system.

I can trace my ancestry back 100 million years, and I do many of the same jobs for Joe today that I've done since the earliest primitive creatures began to appear on earth. Take the matter of temperature control. Thanks to me, Joe can survive in Siberia when the temperature drops as low as -90°F., or in Libya when it climbs to 136°. In either place, I'll keep his internal environment about a steady 98.6°. Let it vary by more than a few degrees either up or down, and Joe would be a goner.

If Joe's blood heats up as little as a tenth of a degree on a warm day, I go to work. I send messages to the pituitary gland and through the sympathetic nervous system to dilate surface blood vessels and open tens of thousands of sweat glands. The sweat cools the skin so as to get rid of the extra heat in Joe's blood. At the same time, I signal other brain areas to speed up breathing so that Joe will pant—and thus carry away more heat.

On the other hand, let Joe's blood temperature drop a tenth of a degree on a cold day, and I cause the adrenal glands and the pituitary to make sure the liver releases more blood sugar as fuel for muscles, which are the main furnaces of the body. I get Joe to start shivering so that heat will be produced by muscle activity. Sweat glands also shut down, detouring blood from body surfaces where it would become further chilled. If Joe is chilled enough, though, surface blood vessels will almost entirely shut down—and he'll turn blue. I do one thing which is rather pointless when he is cold: I give him gooseflesh. This is a hangover from Joe's furry ancestors. For them I used to tighten skin muscles to make their hair stand on end; it produced better insulation that way.

When Joe gets an infection, the bacteria change the sensitivity of my sensors so that the temperature at which they operate is raised to a higher level—as by a thermostat. Joe tries to raise his body temperature to that new level by constriction of surface vessels, and by shivering. When he succeeds, I try to compensate by causing the body to lose heat by sweating and

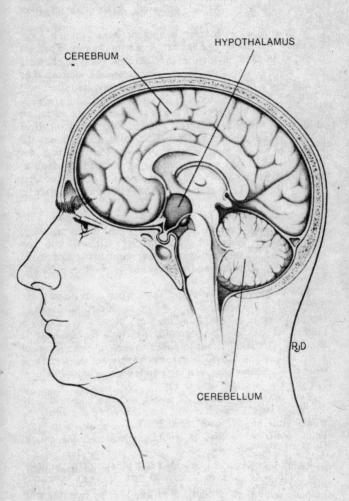

CEREBRUM

HYPOTHALAMUS

CEREBELLUM

dilation of the blood vessels. As Joe gets rid of the infection, my sensors return to normal operating levels and his fever disappears.

Managing water balance is another important job I do. Basically, Joe is a marine animal. As a baby, he was 75 percent water; as an adult, he is closer to 50 percent. Every day he loses about three quarts of moisture via lungs, sweat and urine. If he should lose a fifth or more of his total supply, he'd die.

Hence, too little water calls for emergency action. Once my detectors find blood growing too salty (from lack of water), an antidiuretic hormone (ADH) is released through a joint effort by the pituitary gland and me. The extra ADH causes the kidneys to absorb more water than usual, the urine becomes concentrated and the salivary glands reduce their flow of saliva. Joe's body will now conserve all the water it can, and Joe feels thirsty. He drinks a glass or two of water, and balance is restored.

Suppose his blood becomes *too* watery—as it tends to do when he drinks three or four beers. I signal to the pituitary, which reduces the amount of ADH released into the bloodstream. The kidneys are no longer required to conserve the usual amount of water, and are now able to produce urine at a faster clip.

You would think Joe would know when he is hungry. He doesn't—unless I tell him. Just before mealtime, thousands of bits of information flood in on me. Joe's blood-sugar supply is falling, and mild fatigue is beginning to hit muscles. I evaluate all this and start sending out impulses to step up production of gastric juices and saliva. The stomach increases the speed and force of its contractions, and taste buds become more sensitive. Joe gets the message: time to eat.

Two of my cell groups, or nuclei, seem to be particularly concerned with eating. If one of them should be damaged, Joe would stuff himself with food, not knowing when to stop. Damage the other, and he would immediately stop eating, having lost all interest in food.

Sex is another thing I help take care of. I prod the pituitary into stimulating the gonads; beyond that I don't know exactly how the sex urge is aroused. Although other brain areas play a role, none of us can do the job alone. But without me Joe would be very uncoordinated sexually. Let one of my areas be destroyed and the sex urge disappears. On the other hand, sometimes there is pressure or irritation within the brain which causes me to tell the pituitary to release too much of its sex hormone, which results in an increase in sexual reactivity.

Occasionally, Joe gets into a good-sized rage. As soon as the cortex (the gray matter of the brain) informs me of this, I have a lot to do to prepare Joe for fight or flight—and all at once. I tell the pituitary gland to release hormones that will activate other glands to increase the metabolic rate. To conserve blood that will be needed by muscles, skin vessels constrict while vessels of the muscles dilate. Joe gets pale—but all muscles have a ready supply of blood. Breathing and heartbeat are stepped up, and the amount of blood pumped with each stroke of the heart is increased. Stomach activity decreases, and Joe may find that he must empty his bladder.

There are a few other odds and ends: the cranial nerve prepares the eyes, face muscles, pharynx and heart for a stress response. Muscular tension is increased, skin temperature is lowered and salivary glands are shut down to conserve moisture (Joe's mouth goes dry). As soon as Joe calms down, everything is thrown into reverse—and in a few minutes he's back to normal.

No matter what is going on *outside* Joe, I strive to maintain sameness *inside*. Fortunately, very little ever goes wrong with me. I'm far too well protected to be prone to injury. The main thing I have to worry about is tumors growing in from adjacent areas or a break in the blood supply of the brain.

Can Joe do anything to cut down my work load? Very little. And, really, I don't need any help. I've been around a long time, and I know a lot more about regulating his internal environment than Joe or any other human could ever know.

3
Sensory
Organs

EYE

FOR CONCENTRATED complexities, no other organ in Joe's body can equal me. No larger than a Ping-Pong ball, I have tens of millions of electrical connections and can handle 1.5 million simultaneous messages. I gather 80 percent of all the knowledge Joe absorbs. He thinks of me as a miniature television camera. I consider the comparison insulting. I'm much more sensitive than the biggest, costliest TV camera ever made. I am responsible for one of the greatest of all miracles—sight.

Today's world is giving me a hard time. I wasn't built for it. For Joe's prehistoric ancestors, the eye's main job was to see things at a distance—dangers to be avoided, game to be killed. Only lately have I been called on for continuous close-up work.

Look at my anatomy and you'll understand why I am having difficulty adjusting to today's demands. First, my front window—my clear, dime-size cornea. It starts the seeing process by bending light rays into orderly patterns. Next, my pupil—an adjustable gateway for light. In bright sun it is nearly closed; on a dark night it is wide open. Up to this point there is nothing

Sensory Organs

about seeing that a cheap camera couldn't handle.

My wonders really begin with my lens—a little envelope of fluid the size and shape of an oval vitamin pill. My lens is surrounded by a ring of tiny, superbly strong, unbelievably hard-working muscles. When they tense, my lens fattens for near vision; when they relax, it flattens for distant vision. This was a fine arrangement for Joe's caveman ancestors. Since they were mainly interested in things 20 or more feet away, the muscles were relaxed most of the time. But Joe now lives in a close-up world—lots of reading, desk work and such. This keeps my ciliary muscles tensed a lot of the time. They grow tired.

In front of and behind my lens I have two fluid-filled chambers. In front the fluid is like water; in back it is about the consistency of egg white. The watery fluid keeps me firmly inflated. Both fluids must be absolutely clear to permit passage of light. Those "specks" Joe sees when he looks at a bright light are cellular remnants left over from his days in the womb when I was under construction. They will float aimlessly in his eye fluid as long as he lives.

When Joe looks at some object, the light passes through my lens, which brings it into correct focus on my retina, a kind of onionskin wallpaper which covers the rear two thirds of my interior. Except in Joe's brain, I don't think that anywhere else in his body is so much packed into so small a space. Covering less than a square inch, my retina contains 137 *million* light-sensitive receptor cells: 130 million shaped like rods for black-and-white vision, seven million shaped like cones for color vision.

The rods are scattered all over my retina. Let a firefly pass at night and a complex chemistry gets under way. The faint light bleaches rhodopsin, a purplish-red pigment in my rods. The bleaching process generates a tiny wisp of electricity—a few millionths of a volt, far too little to tickle a mosquito. This feeds into my straw-size optic nerve and is transmitted to Joe's brain at about 300 miles per hour. The brain interprets the signals flooding in and hands down its verdict: a firefly. All of this intricate electrochemical activity has been completed in about .002 second!

If my rods seem complex, my cones are far more so. They are

concentrated in the fovea, a pinhead-size, yellowish depression at the rear of my chamber. This is the center for acute vision—reading, any close work—and for color. A leading theory is that these cones, too, have bleachable pigments, one each for red, green and blue. Like an artist mixing paints on a palette, Joe's brain blends these colors to make scores of other hues. If anything should go wrong with this intricate electrochemical process, Joe would be color-blind—as one in eight men is to some degree. In dim light, activity of my cones diminishes, color sense vanishes and everything becomes gray, as my rods take over.

While Joe sees *with* me, he sees *in* his brain. A crushing blow at the back of his head, severe enough to destroy the optical center of his brain, would produce permanent blindness. A lesser blow and he sees "stars'—a chaotic electrical disturbance. Joe gets clinching evidence of the brain's role when he dreams. He "sees" pictures, even with my lids closed in total darkness. Had he been born blind, he would dream in terms of other sensory stimuli: touch, sound, even smell.

Joe wasn't born with the eyes he has today. At birth, he could see only light and shadow. In the first few months he was farsighted, like his caveman ancestors. To study his rattle, he held it as far as possible from his face. At first, Joe's eyes were poorly coordinated; I'd wander in one direction, my partner in another. Our wandering worried Joe's mother. It shouldn't have. A few months after birth we were moving in exact unison. By the time Joe was six, his vision was excellent. But my peak sight didn't come until age eight.

When he was young, Joe used to read in dim light. His mother warned that he was "ruining" his eyes. Nonsense. The young see better in dim light than adults; and viewing under even the most adverse circumstances does no harm.

I have a number of other unusual attributes. Tiny though they are, my muscles, milligram for milligram, are among the body's strongest. In an average day, I move about 100,000 times—to bring objects into sharp focus. Joe would have to walk 50 miles to give his leg muscles similar exercise.

My cleaning equipment is similarly striking. My lacrimal glands produce a steady stream of moisture—tears to flush away

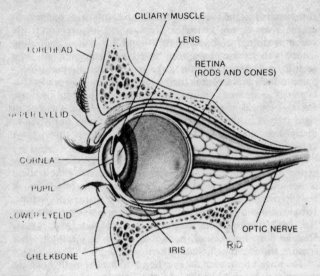

dust and other foreign material. My eyelids, of course, act as windshield wipers. Joe blinks three to six times a minute—more when I am tired. This keeps my cornea moist and clean. The tears also contain a potent microbe-killer called lysozyme, which guards me from infective bacteria.

I try to ward off fatigue by resting as much as possible. I get time off when Joe blinks. And my partner and I spell each other: for a while I may carry 90 percent of the work load, while Joe's other eye loafs; then it goes to work and I rest.

Nature gave me superb protection, placing me in a bony cavern with protruding cheekbones and forehead to act as shock absorbers for direct blows. She also gave me supersensitive nerves to activate the alarm if there should be a potentially damaging intruder such as a cinder.

Still, I do have my troubles. My focusing apparatus often fails to work perfectly. Eyeglasses can correct 95 percent of this trouble. Disease is a more serious problem. One potential disorder is really a plumbing problem—either too much fluid entering me or too little draining away. Pressure builds up, reducing the blood supply to my optic nerve. This is glaucoma.

In severe instances, glaucoma can cause permanent blindness in a few days. More often it is a leisurely performer, producing symptoms so mild they are apt to go unnoticed. These symptoms: colored halos around bright lights, loss of side vision, difficulty in adjusting to the dark, a blurring of vision. At his age, Joe has one chance in 40 of glaucoma damaging his sight or blinding him completely. His doctor can check for glaucoma simply by pressing a little gadget called a tonometer against my eyeball. Joe should have this test every year. The treatment for glaucoma? Drugs in drop form, or surgery.

Astigmatism is another of my common ailments. In this one, my cornea is not a spherical surface and distorts vision like a bubble flaw in a piece of glass. Eyeglasses correct this condition. A detached retina is more serious. It occurs when my retinal wallpaper blisters or peels, and usually announces itself with flashing lights, image distortion, blurring spots. A surgeon can "tack" my wallpaper back in place with 80 percent chance of success.

Both my cornea and my lens—normally totally transparent tissue—can cloud and lead to blindness. If it's the cornea, Joe can regain sight with a corneal transplant. If it's the lens, he will need a cataract operation, and either thick eyeglasses or contact lenses afterward.

Fortunately, Joe has so far escaped all these things. Just the same, I am growing old—like Joe's other organs. The transparency of my lens is lower, accommodation muscles are weaker, hardened arteries are diminishing blood supply to my retina. These processes will continue, but Joe shouldn't worry unduly. The odds are heavily in favor of my providing him with serviceable vision as long as he lives.

EAR

JOE IS IMPRESSED by the computer his company bought not long ago. It will perform seeming miracles, but to me it is as crude as a concrete mixer. Perhaps I am prejudiced, for I am a triumph of miniaturization. Nowhere in his body is so much crammed into so small a space as in me. I have enough electrical circuits to provide phone service for a good-sized city. I am also a kind of automatic pilot, keeping Joe from toppling over.

I am Joe's right ear, and I do all this in a space not much larger than a hazelnut! Joe considers his eyes his most important sensory organs. Yet, without my partner and me, he would be doomed to solitary sonic confinement—far more emotionally disabling than blindness.

Joe thinks of me simply as that flap of tissue on the side of his head. This outer ear, however, is nothing but a sound-gathering trumpet. From it, a one-inch canal runs obliquely to the eardrum, twisting to protect my delicate inner components and warming air to keep things cozy. In this canal, a profusion of hairs and 4000 wax glands act as a flypaper trap for insects, dust and other potential irritants. Further, the wax guards against infection, particularly when Joe swims in dirty water. (He can wash away unsightly wax, but I wish he wouldn't pick at the rest—he could harm my eardrum, and I'll shed excess wax naturally.)

My eardrum, a tough, tightly stretched membrane less than half an inch across, is where the intricate business of hearing starts. Sound-bearing airwaves strike it—like a stick beating a drum. Even faint vibrations from a whisper can push it inward—but ever so little, perhaps only a billionth of a centimeter. This minute displacement is then changed, in an awe-inspiring chain of events not yet entirely understood, into meaningful sound for Joe.

To see how, step through my drumhead to Joe's bean-size middle ear. Here are hinged together three tiny bones called the anvil, hammer and stirrup (also known as the stapes) because they vaguely resemble those things. It is their job to step up the tiny movements of my drum, amplifying them 22 times and passing them on to my inner ear via an oval window attached to the stirrup.

My inner ear—the *real* organ of hearing—resides in a fortresslike cavern hollowed out of the body's hardest bone and filled with watery fluid. Its major hearing component is the snail-shaped cochlea, whose twisting interior is studded with thousands of microscopic hairlike nerve cells, each one tuned to a particular vibration. When the middle ear's stirrup "knocks" on the oval window leading to the inner ear, this fluid is set vibrating. If middle C has been sounded, say, then the cochlea's middle C's hair cell vibrates, waving in the lymph fluid like seaweed in a tidal current.

The waving produces a wisp of electricity that feeds into my auditory nerve (only the diameter of a pencil lead, this nerve contains more than 30,000 circuits!), which in turn leads to Joe's brain, three fourths of an inch away. My cochlea may feed in thousands of electrical messages, with Joe's left ear doing the same. It's the brain's job to unscramble these data and convert them into meaningful sound. Thus, Joe hears *with* me, but *in* his brain.

So far I've talked only of sound conducted by airwaves. Joe

Sensory Organs

can also hear by bone conduction. When Joe speaks, part of the sound leaves his mouth and strikes my drum, but another part travels directly to my inner-ear fluid via the jawbones. Thus, what Joe hears is quite different from what a listener hears. That's why he has trouble recognizing his own voice on a tape recorder. It's also why Joe thinks he is making quite a racket when he eats celery.

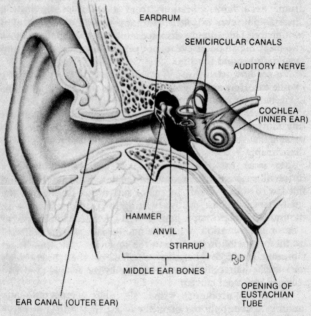

EARDRUM

SEMICIRCULAR CANALS

AUDITORY NERVE

COCHLEA (INNER EAR)

HAMMER

ANVIL

STIRRUP

MIDDLE EAR BONES

OPENING OF EUSTACHIAN TUBE

EAR CANAL (OUTER EAR)

But hearing is only part of the story of my miraculous inner ear. Above the cochlea I have three minute, fluid-filled semicircular canals. These loops of tubing are Joe's organ of balance. One detects up-and-down motion, another forward motion, the third lateral motion. If Joe starts to fall, fluid in one of my canals is displaced. Hair cells there detect this and inform Joe's brain, which orders muscles to tighten to keep him upright.

As a youngster, Joe sometimes liked to be whirled by another boy until he was staggering. What happened was this: fluid in the canals was being displaced so rapidly that the brain was getting more messages than it could handle, and Joe lost all muscular control. Let disorderly displacement of fluid continue too long, as in a tossing boat, and I begin to involve other organs. Joe breaks into a sweat, and motion sickness is apt to follow.

Joe's hearing started declining almost the moment he was born. It is now going down each year as my tissues lose elasticity, hair cells degenerate and calcium deposits invade critical spots. When Joe was a baby, he had a hearing range of 16 to 30,000 cycles per second (vibrations). (If it had gone much below 16 he could have heard the vibrations of his own body. As a matter of fact, Joe *can* hear his body vibrations. Let him stopper his ears with his fingers: the low rumble he hears comes from tensed finger and arm muscles.) By the time he reached his teens, the upper limit of his hearing had dropped to 20,000 cycles. Now he hears nothing above 8000, and, if he reaches the age of 80, that will be down to about 4000. He will then hear conversation reasonably well in a quiet place, but may have difficulty in a noisy area. He will hear low tones better than high tones.

He also has a decibel loss. Decibels measure sound *intensity* at any particular frequency. Thus, a whisper from four feet away in a quiet room ranks at about 30 decibels, normal conversation about 60, a rock band 120, and a shotgun 140. (But this doesn't mean that a rock band is only twice as loud as normal conversation. A jump of twenty points on the tricky decibel scale means a hundredfold increase of intensity.) Right now Joe has a 40-decibel loss; his hearing is quite serviceable, but he is beginning to ask people to repeat words.

With any structure as complex as mine, a great deal can go wrong. Drum punctures are frequent—fortunately, most such punctures heal themselves or can be repaired by an operation. Tinnitus, or ringing in the ears, is another source of trouble. This can be caused by almost anything: drugs (some antibiotics, alcohol), fever, circulation changes, tumors on my acoustic nerve. Once the causative factor is tracked down and eliminated, I sometimes cease my racket.

Middle-ear infections are another source of trouble—and,

before antibiotics, often culminated in hearing loss. The eustachian tube, leading from the middle ear to Joe's throat, is the culprit. The throat is, microbially speaking, a very dirty place, and the eustachian tube offers microbes easy access to the middle ear. When he has a cold, Joe would be wise not to blow his nose too hard—it forces throat pollution into me.

Sometimes an overgrowth of bone is apt to freeze motion of the bones in my middle ear. Once motion stops, hearing is impaired. This is conduction deafness. Joe has the beginnings of it, but chances of its progressing to really serious deafness are only about one in ten. If this happens, Joe has two options: a hearing aid or surgery. The operation (which has an 80 percent chance of success) replaces my stirrup bone with a tiny filament of stainless steel. Motion of the bones resumes, and Joe can hear again.

Perhaps the biggest thing Joe should be worrying about right now is noise pollution. Joe knows that workers in noisy trades may develop hearing difficulty, and that today's rock musicians will probably be wearing hearing aids a few years hence. But he thinks *he* can adjust to today's shrill racket. He can't. When excessively loud, low-pitched sounds strike my drum, I have muscles to tighten it; otherwise, I take what comes. This was fine for Joe's ancestors. Thunder or the roar of a lion were the loudest sounds around, and these were low-pitched. It's the new high-pitched sounds—such as the whine of jets, the rat-a-tat-tat of riveting machines—that wreck me.

Sustained loud noise can wreck internal organs of a mouse and eventually kill it. If such an experiment were ever tried on Joe, I can guess the result. What can Joe do about it? He could speak out against senseless noise, seek quiet in home and office and cover his ears when he goes hunting—the repeated burst of a shotgun can *really* wreck me. He could stop smoking, or at least cut down. Nicotine (coffee, too) constricts arteries in my all-important inner ear, reducing the nourishment my inner ear needs.

Joe has his eyes examined regularly, and I would like the same attention. If Joe only knew how limited and lonely the world of silence is, he would take all possible steps to preserve my partner and me.

NOSE

I AM THAT LITTLE hill that rises from the center of Joe's face—his nose. He worries about his eyes, ears and digestive tract but tends to think of me as a nuisance. I water on winter days, sneeze at the wrong time, clog with a cold, tend to get smashed in accidents. There are colorful and poetic allusions to other facial features—eyes, ears, lips. But not to me. I am kept to the grindstone, one pays through me, and nothing is plainer than the nose on a face.

But I am an important organ in Joe's body, and do numerous jobs that he is unaware of. Let him go to sleep on his left side, for example, and my left nostril will gradually become engorged. In about two hours I send out a silent signal—I don't want to awaken him—which causes him to turn over. This is one of several trigger mechanisms that lead to movement, preventing his muscles from being cramped in the morning.

Automatically, I sniff Joe's victuals before he eats, to protect him from spoiled food that might poison him. Much of Joe's pleasure in eating comes through me. Let me smell a broiling steak and I crank up salivary glands that set his mouth to watering and start his digestive juices flowing. As Joe has noticed, when my capabilities are blunted by sickness, as by a cold, his food is tasteless, and he loses appetite and weight. Without my stimulus Joe becomes a picky eater.

Another thing. Joe has a pleasing, deep voice. In part he has me to thank. I contribute some resonance. Let him pinch his nostrils when he speaks and possibly he'll hear the difference I make.

Architecturally, I am nothing to boast about. I am sandwiched in between the roof of Joe's mouth and his brain. In reality, I am *two* noses, since a septum, or partition, divides me in two. Above Joe's mouth I have a rather cavernous interior, my workroom. I also have small hollows in the bones on each side—in the cheeks, in the frontal bone over the eyes, in the wall between me and the eyes, and at the back of my main cavity. These hollow spaces make up my eight sinuses. They contribute some of the moisture I need to humidify air, make a slight contribution to voice quality and lighten Joe's skull, but mostly they cause trouble. Bacteria slip in to cause infection and blockage of the narrow channels that empty into my main passages. Then Joe is in for painful, headachy misery.

One of my major tasks is cleaning and conditioning the air for Joe's lungs. Each day I must process about 500 cubic feet of air—a small roomful. Joe may be skiing on a frigid, dry day, but his lungs aren't interested in dry, zero air. They want about what one would find on a humid summer day—75 to 80 percent saturated, temperature in the 90s. They demand air almost totally free of bacteria, and cleansed of grit, smoke and other irritants. The air conditioner for a medium-sized room is as large as a small trunk. My air-conditioning system is compressed into a tiny area only a few inches long.

For the humidifying job I secrete about a quart of moisture a day. Mostly this is sticky mucus, produced by the spongy, red membrane that lines my passages. While the rough cleaning job is done by hairs in Joe's nostrils, it's the mucus that does the major work, acting as a kind of flypaper to trap bacteria and particles that get past the hairs. Naturally, I can't permit this film of mucus to stagnate. In a few hours there would be total

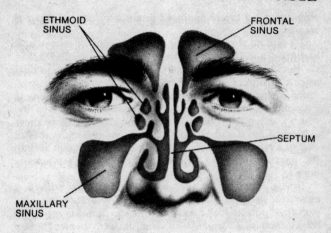

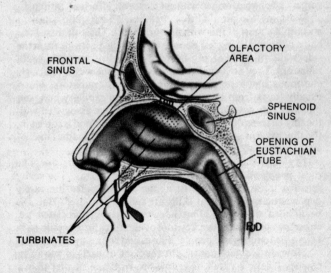

pollution. So every 20 minutes I produce a clean new mucous blanket.

To remove the old mucus, I have an army of microscopic brooms—cilia. These minute hairs rapidly whip the film back to the throat for swallowing and then slowly settle back to their original positions. Strong stomach acid destroys most swallowed bacteria. My tireless little cilia make about ten sweeping strokes a second. Joe, of course, is unaware of this activity, which goes on day and night. But on a cold day he becomes aware of it, since cold partially paralyzes my cilia and causes an overproduction of mucus. Then, instead of being swept back to the throat, the moisture dribbles out the front. Joe gets a runny nose.

Besides mechanical trapping I have another protection against bacteria—a microbe slayer called lysozyme, the same stuff that protects Joe's eyes from infection. It makes me one of the cleanest of all organs—so clean, in fact, that much nose surgery can be performed without elaborate efforts at antisepsis.

Warming the air that Joe breathes is also quite a task. I accomplish most of this with my turbinates. Three of these little chips of bone, the biggest about an inch long, protrude from the side walls of each of my nostrils. In reality, they are small radiators. They are covered with erectile tissue with a relatively enormous blood supply—the steam for my radiators. Blood usually flows from tiny arteries, through a capillary bed, and into veins. In my turbinates the capillaries are associated with the tiny cisterns of my erectile tissue. As more blood is forced in, the tiny caverns swell. This happens when Joe breathes in cold air—I swell and provide greater warming surface.

My other big job, of course, is detection of odors. Joe, like most people, can recognize 4000 different scents. The really sensitive nose can go up to about 10,000. Since life rarely depends on me, my great skills are subdued, unused. Had Joe been born deaf and blind he would have appreciated my enormous potential. As a key tool of identification I would have been able to recognize people, houses and rooms by scent alone.

How do I detect odors? On the roof of each of my nasal cavities I have a patch of yellow-brown tissue smaller than a postage stamp. In each patch I have roughly ten million receptor cells, and six to eight tiny sensory hairs that project from each cell. All this apparatus is connected to Joe's brain, an inch away.

That, then, is the setup. But it doesn't tell *how* Joe identifies the smell of a broiling steak. We have only theories. It's known that anything smellable throws off molecules. Hot onion soup throws them off in plenty, cold steel hardly any at all. One theory holds that my receptor sites can distinguish the sizes and shapes of different molecules. The difference is somehow registered, and a wisp of electricity is generated and dispatched to the brain. The electrical signal is familiar to Joe's brain. The brain arrives at a verdict: vinegar, it says, or marigold or burning rubber.

Actually, it isn't all that simple. It is possible that there are primary odors, just as there are three primary colors. With the brain as a palette, odors are blended into a familiar scent.

If I am overwhelmed by a particular odor, after a short time I can no longer detect it. After the first few whiffs, Joe's wife hardly notices the perfume she is wearing. If Joe gets a job in a tannery, glueworks or stockyard, he is oppressed by the odors at first. Soon, however, he is so worn out with those particular harsh smells that he hardly notices them. Yet his sensitivity to other odors remains. Even in the stench of a tannery a rose smells as sweet as ever.

As one of the body's most exposed organs, it's little wonder that I am the target for a wide spectrum of ailments. Certain microbes—notably those of syphilis and tuberculosis—can attack my cartilage and destroy my shape. Polyps sprout on my mucous membrane—little "mushrooms" that vary from pea to grape size. They can block air passages or sinus channels to cause a variety of grief.

Allergens, tobacco smoke and dust irritate my mucous membranes, causing them to swell and to produce excess fluid which drips into the throat. This is postnasal drip. Or air passages may be inflamed and shut by a cold. Joe often tries to blast them open with a mighty blow. This is dangerous business. It can force infection into my sinuses, or into the middle ear via the eustachian tubes. Or he may resort to nose drops—tissue shrinkers of various kinds. He'd best be cautious here, too. Drops cause the "rebound" phenomenon—temporary shrinkage is followed by greater swelling than was originally present.

39

Sensory Organs

Experts warn against nose drops because they end by complicating rather than solving the problem.

Joe is 47 now and my acuity is declining. Coffee doesn't smell quite as good as it once did, and other odors aren't quite as noxious. All this is perfectly normal. It might have been a handicap at one point in man's development, but no longer. Until I warm and cleanse Joe's last breath I will continue to do my jobs for him. And in defense of my lowly status I might add that in Joe's old age I will do my jobs far better than his eyes and ears will do theirs.

SKIN

JOE THINKS OF ME, his skin, as a not too interesting sausage wrapper, an inert parchment demanding much—shaving, bathing, scratching, anointing—and giving little. How wrong he is. I am an absolute essential.

I do jobs he never dreamed of. He doesn't think of me as a manufacturer of intricate chemicals, but I am. I produce at least one important vitamin—vitamin D—and activate the sex hormone, testosterone, produced by Joe's testes. I help regulate blood pressure. I keep water in (Joe would quickly die if I didn't); I also keep water *out* (Joe can swim for hours without becoming waterlogged). My complex nervous system detects pain, touch, heat, cold, and instantly passes findings along to Joe's brain. I have been called the "frontier" of Joe's body. But maybe "rampart" would be better, for I protect against a mighty horde of potentially deadly invaders—bacteria—that live or land on my surface.

I come in many forms—Joe's fingernails and toenails, the hair on his head, the callus on his sole, the wart he once had on a finger. And I am made up of three layers: the outer *epidermis*,

41

the middle *dermis*, the bottom *subcutaneous* tissue.

In most places around Joe's body my outer layer is paper-thin. He can see for himself next time he burns a finger: my epidermis is the transparent tissue on the top of the blister. Joe can shave off a callus without a bloodletting because there is no blood supply in my epidermis. Its cells are nourished by diffusion from below.

While a snake sheds its skin in dramatic fashion, the shedding of my epidermis is a slow, steady process. Each day many millions of baby epidermal cells are formed in the innermost part of my epidermis and begin pushing their way outward, changing as they go—from jellylike cellular material to harder, horny *keratin*. My keratin layer consists of flattened, shingly cells—all dead. (Fragile living cells couldn't survive exposed to the hostile outside.) Each day millions are washed away when Joe showers, or are rubbed away by clothing. Thus Joe gets a new outer skin every 27 days—the birth-to-death span of these cells.

Functionally, there isn't a great deal to be said for my fatty subcutaneous portion. It acts as a shock absorber to protect internal organs, serves as an insulator to conserve body heat and is responsible for pleasing body contours—more important to women than to men. Some experts don't consider this layer part of me at all—subcutaneous actually means *"beneath* the skin."

Look now at my tough "hide," or dermis. It is the strong but elastic envelope that holds everything together—that keeps vessels, fat, etc., from bulging or falling out. The dermis contains an intricate collection of nerves, blood vessels and glands. The mix varies at different places in Joe's body. But under an average square centimeter of surface—an area the size of Joe's little fingernail and about 1/8 inch thick—there will be some 100 sweat glands, 12 feet of nerves, hundreds of nerve endings, 10 hair follicles, 15 sebaceous glands and 3 feet of blood vessels!

My intricate network of blood vessels is particularly interesting. Let Joe exercise on a hot day and these blood vessels dilate; he becomes flushed. I am trying to radiate heat to the outside to get rid of it. On a cold day the reverse takes place. My vessels shut down, detouring blood to the interior of Joe's body; he goes pale. My blood vessels are also under the command of emotions. When angry, Joe flushes—I've opened up the blood vessels of his face. Fear shuts them down—Joe gets cold feet.

It's no news, of course, that evaporation of sweat cools the body. But that hardly tells the full story of my complex air-conditioning system. Let body temperature vary more than a few degrees from a normal 98.6° F., and Joe is a goner. To avoid this, I have a staggering number of sweat glands—two million, spread around Joe's 18 square feet of body surface. Each is a tightly coiled little tube buried deep in my dermis, with a 50-inch-long duct rising to the surface. Tiny as they are, I have a total of six *miles* of these ducts.

Extracting water, salt and some wastes from the blood, my sweat glands function almost continuously. On a day of comfortable temperature, when Joe isn't even aware that he is sweating, my glands will produce half a pint of water. But if Joe

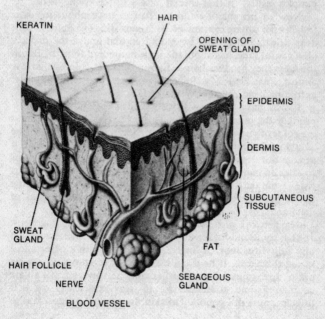

KERATIN

HAIR

OPENING OF SWEAT GLAND

EPIDERMIS

DERMIS

SUBCUTANEOUS TISSUE

SWEAT GLAND

HAIR FOLLICLE

NERVE

BLOOD VESSEL

FAT

SEBACEOUS GLAND

were a professional football lineman, playing on a hot day, he might lose seven quarts—that's about 14 pounds of water.

My sweat glands also respond to emotional stimuli. In periods of anxiety Joe breaks out into what he calls a "cold" sweat—it's cold because there are quantities of it subject to rapid evaporation. With fear, his palms get damp—again, excessive production.

Of more dubious value are my sebaceous or fat glands—several hundred thousand of them, producers of a semiliquid oil. Mostly they are attached to hair follicles, and lubricate both the hair and surrounding skin. For Joe's primitive hair-covered ancestors, these glands probably served a useful purpose: keeping hair waterproof, and enhancing its heat-retaining capability. Today they mainly cause trouble. My hair follicles become clogged, cellular debris collects and blackheads and pimples result—or that special misery of the young, acne.

Now to my manufacture of hair. I have about ten hair follicles per square centimeter, each consisting of a bulbous root deep down, and a shaft extending up and above the surface. (Joe's wife, Jane, has about the same number of follicles. But in the main they produce hair so fine and so light-colored that it is almost invisible.) My follicles produce hair continuously, extruding dead cells above the surface.

I also have millions of cells called melanocytes, which produce the pigment melanin. This is the stuff that determines the color of Joe's hair, eyes and skin. (If it were lacking in Joe, he would be an albino.) Melanin is mainly a protective substance; it screens out dangerous ultraviolet from the sun's rays. A day or so after Joe has been out in the sun, my pigment granules start rising from the lower part of my epidermis to the surface, giving him a protective tan. Freckles are simply concentrations of melanin.

My network of nerves is really awesome. On his fingertips, Joe has thousands of sensory nerve endings per square inch. Let him stub a toe, burn a finger, nick himself with a razor and I sound the alarm. If he is chilled, my cold receptors inform his brain. Joe's muscles go to work and he shivers to stimulate circulation, and gooseflesh forms—tiny muscles in my hair follicles cause this pebbling of skin. Its original purpose was to make hairs stand erect—providing greater protection when fighting, greater warmth when cold. Today this still works for Joe's dog, but not for Joe.

Joe is 47 years old and I am beginning to show signs of age. Typically, with age I become thinner, more transparent (veins in the hands of the aged become prominent). My undercoat of fat diminishes and, as it does, wrinkles form. Elastic skin fibers lose snap: bags begin to form under eyes, jowls begin to sag.

The biggest danger I face is cancer. Mostly this traces to overexposure to the sun (which also ages skin). Forehead, nose and ears are favorite spots. Fortunately, my cancers are highly curable. But they can be killers, so Joe would do well to take heed of any growths on his skin—especially if they bleed and don't heal.

Can Joe do anything for me? Avoiding overexposure to the sun is perhaps the most important thing—down to wearing a hat when he plays golf. Unless skin is unduly oily, excessive tub soaking is bad in wintry weather since it dries me out.

No matter how good the care Joe gives me, I will still cause him a certain amount of trouble. Since I am the bulwark between inside and outside, totally exposed and subject to trouble from both within and without, it isn't surprising that I am prey to an array of diseases—upward of 2000. Psoriasis is a major one. Its red, scaly patches are caused by epidermis cells being formed and discarded too rapidly—perhaps in five days rather than a normal 27. Cause? No one knows. Shingles is another of my banes. This one is caused by the chickenpox virus. First comes pain, often a great deal. Then blisters form—usually, but not always, in the trunk area. The pain may persist, especially in older people, for some time after the blisters heal.

In cases of these and other diseases, Joe will just have to get his doctor's advice, and be thankful that I do as well as I do.

TONGUE

FROM TIME TO TIME, Joe sticks me out and examines me in the mirror. He is not exactly sure what he is looking for. If he finds anything unusual, he is almost certain to misinterpret it. That is about the end of his interest in me. After all, I'm only four inches long and weigh but two ounces, and I usually stay out of sight. I am Joe's tongue.

Compared with the eyes and ears, I have had a bad press: my faculty of taste has been called the "poor cousin of the five senses." Unfair, I say! Let Joe try to get along without me! Let him extend me from his mouth, for instance, and clamp me lightly between his teeth, and then try to speak. What comes out is hardly recognizable.

True, I don't have the virtuosity of some animal tongues. I can't flick out to catch insects the way a frog's tongue does, or "feel" the way through a dark cavern as a serpent's tongue can. Just the same, I have a large assortment of jobs: I assist in mastication, rolling food around in the mouth so that it is evenly ground and made acceptable to the stomach. I am quite a serviceable toothpick—I like to keep my domain clean of debris of all sorts. I even express emotions: Joe's children stick out their tongues to indicate aversion or disgust.

One of my most important—and complex—tasks is to assist in swallowing. For this, my front part presses against the hard palate in the roof of the mouth. Then my rear portion humps up, catapulting food into the passage which leads to the esophagus. Though it sounds quite simple, it is actually a symphony of activity, conducted by nerves and executed by intricate muscles. Joe knew how to swallow before he emerged from the womb—an indication of how critical the swallowing reflex is to life.

Speech is another matter. I had to be trained for this extraordinary neuromuscular feat. As a baby, Joe experimented with sounds for more than two years before he was able to form simple sentences. Today, I am a tireless gymnast, able to flex myself into a great variety of shapes for more complex expression. Joe can get some idea of my acrobatics by uttering a single sentence. As he speaks, let him concentrate on my motions. He will be amazed at the activity.

Or, he can give thought to another matter. I live in constant proximity to a very real enemy—the teeth. They are capable of doing me real injury. But I am an extremely artful dodger; I keep out of their way and am rarely bitten.

Essentially, I am a slab of mucous membrane enclosing a complex array of muscles and nerves. My upper surface is studded with papillae—little nipples, some of which contain taste buds. Located in my taste buds are taste cells, which actually receive the sensation of taste. On my underside is a tiny cord, the frenulum. Let this cord be too short, restraining normal motion, and I am tongue-tied. Victims once went through life with garbled speech. Today, this defect can be corrected by surgery.

My taste buds look something like microscopic rosebuds. Their tasting action is a chemical process, like smell. Curiously enough, they are on my under as well as my upper side. Until recently, scientists thought that they had my taste buds completely mapped: I tasted salt with my tip, sweet in the middle, bitter in the rear and sour along my sides. (These are four of the basic tastes. And just as the primary colors red, blue and yellow blend into a thousand hues, so too do the basic tastes blend into thousands of taste sensations.) But the researchers were wrong.

Taste buds are by no means confined to me, but are scattered around Joe's oral cavity. The primary tasters of sour and bitter are near the junction of the soft and hard palates in the roof of the mouth. If Joe ever wears dentures that cover his palate, these buds will be covered up and things won't taste so good. Lemon pie will lose some of its sour tang, and tea and coffee may become less flavorsome without their predominant bitterness. Most of the buds for salt and sweet *are* on the tongue—although a few are elsewhere, particularly in the upper throat.

Food must be liquefied before any real taste emerges. This is true even of ice cream, which, until it melts in the mouth, is quite tasteless. But once liquefied, it binds to the sweet-taste receptors of the buds; a minute electrochemical current is generated and passed by cranial nerves to the gustatory terminals in the brain. (Other impulses are transmitted for foods that taste sour, bitter or salty.) Like colors mixed on a palette, the messages are blended, and the brain hands down its verdict: the ice cream is delicious.

For a long time, it was assumed that all foods tasted alike to all people. (It's a strange notion when you think about it—everyone knows that hearing and sight are subject to great variations.) Now it becomes clearer all the time that there are vast differences in taste sensitivity. To one person, spinach may be honestly delicious; to another, bitter and horrid. It's the same with scores of other foods. Several pure chemicals point up variations in human taste response. Sodium benzoate, for example, is sweet to some, and to others sour, bitter, salty or tasteless. So there's no point in arguing if someone doesn't like the Roquefort cheese that you find delectable.

Indications are that taste follows regular inheritance patterns. Just the same, tongues do have a certain amount of adaptability, and Joe has learned to accept foods that he once found intolerable. Few babies like buttermilk; many adults do. It took time for me to learn to accept such things as curry, chili and strong cheese. And once I've learned I don't forget: unlike most other organs of the body, I hold up well with age. Joe's sight and hearing will diminish, but not his taste—bean soup has

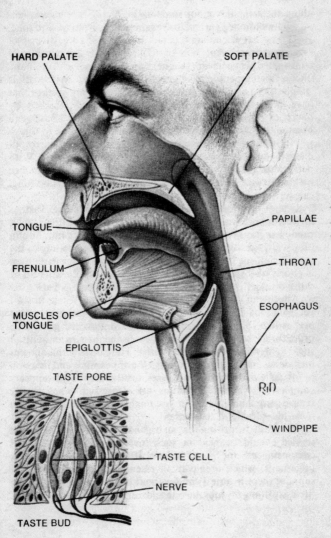

HARD PALATE

SOFT PALATE

TONGUE

PAPILLAE

FRENULUM

THROAT

MUSCLES OF TONGUE

ESOPHAGUS

EPIGLOTTIS

WINDPIPE

TASTE PORE

TASTE CELL

NERVE

TASTE BUD

49

about the same flavor for someone at 90 as when he was ten.

As I mentioned earlier, Joe examines me from time to time. He thinks that when I am "coated" it's a sign of a digestive upset or constipation. Not necessarily. Many of the chronically constipated have clear tongues, and the tongues of many unconstipated people have greenish-white coats. My "coat" is simply tiny particles of food and old cells on my surface that have been trapped between my papillae and attacked by microbes (all of which can be scrubbed away). Those who breathe through their mouths are particularly prone to this.

Nevertheless, the tongue has been called the "mirror of disease" and often gives evidence of trouble elsewhere. With pernicious anemia, I am often red, beefy, smooth; jaundice makes me yellowish; with pellagra, I'm fiery red. Certain fungi can turn me black.

One of my more unpleasant ailments is dysgeusia. Taste is distorted; sugar can be repugnant, meat may taste dreadful. A candy bar may taste salty or a mackerel sweet. This common and now widely recognized disorder seems to be due mainly to the shortage of zinc in the body. The zinc is either lacking in the diet, is poorly absorbed or is lost in large amounts following flu or other diseases. Increase the supply and taste comes back.

Another of my ills is hypogeusia, which decreases the flavor I get from food and drink. Most foods are simply tasteless—roast beef is like soft rubber, an orange like unflavored gelatin. In order for me to taste sweetness, Joe must heap extra amounts of sugar in his morning cereal and coffee. The causes of this ailment include several factors that change the appearance and function of my taste buds. In extreme cases, taste perception disappears completely. Naturally, victims are depressed. They finally realize something the rest of you might note: taste is one of the most pleasurable of the senses.

It is really surprising that an organ that gives people so much service should be held in such low esteem. Under normal circumstances, Joe gives me less attention than his hair or fingernails, which aren't at all essential to his well-being. I suppose there is little I can do about it—except go right along tirelessly doing my jobs, tasting and talking my way through life.

4
Glands
of Internal
Secretion

PITUITARY

I AM A PINKISH, pea-size nubbin of tissue. I hang, like a cherry, on a tiny stem from the underside of Joe's brain. I weigh only about 1/50 of an ounce—and 85 percent of that is water. But after Joe's brain I am probably the most complex organ in his body. I play a key role in almost everything that Joe is or does.

The all-important hormones that I secrete can work wonders or wreak havoc. I can let Joe live a perfectly normal existence, I can sicken him with a bizarre spectrum of diseases—or I can kill him. It was one of my hormones that gave Joe his initial push into the world: oxytocin started the contractions of his mother's womb. It was I who decided that he should be of normal size, rather than a three-foot midget or an eight-foot giant. I can shrink his sexual organs back to boy size, or so hasten his aging process that he will be an old man in a few months' time. I am Joe's pituitary gland.

I have been described as Joe's master gland, the conductor of his endocrine symphony. I take my orders straight from that prune-size section of Joe's brain called the hypothalamus, from

Glands of Internal Secretion

which I hang. It is my job to monitor the activity of other glands, to see that they produce exactly the right amounts of *their* hormones. I suppose you could call me a chemical boss of Joe's body. And I'm not bragging when I call myself the earth's most compact and intricate chemical plant.

I am divided into two lobes. My small posterior lobe stores two hormones produced by the hypothalamus. My much larger anterior lobe produces a probable ten hormones—no one is quite sure. These hormones are among the most complex substances known to man. My total daily output, however, is less than $1/1,000,000$ of a gram.

It took a long time to pry the first of my secrets from me. For centuries, doctors thought my function a lowly one: I was believed to be the source of nasal mucus! My elusive secretions were present in far too small quantities to be detected until the advent of modern chemistry. Now they are being found by accumulating large quantities of different animal and human pituitaries.

One of my hormones manages the thyroid gland in Joe's neck. If I should secrete too much of this thyrotropic hormone, thereby setting too fast a pace for the thyroid, Joe would almost literally burn up. His appetite would be wolfish, yet he would remain rail-thin. On the other hand, if I were to produce too little of this hormone, he would be sluggish, puffy, dim-witted. Fortunately, I have a built-in feedback mechanism to prevent either of these things from happening.

Much of the same situation exists with Joe's testicles. I have two hormones which govern these glands—one by stimulating production of sperm cells and male hormone, the other by promoting growth of the duct system to transport the sperm. Incidentally, Joe's wife has identical hormones to nudge along development of her ovaries and production of eggs. Thus, fertility—and life—depend on me.

For Joe's wife, I normally secrete only enough follicle-stimulating hormone (FSH) and interstitial-cell-stimulating hormone (ICSH) to produce a single mature egg a month. If I were to go on a spree and produce too much FSH and ICSH, five or more eggs might ripen in a single month, and Jane might have quintuplets. It's the same with Joe's testes: too little FSH and ICSH, and he would become fretful, whining and sexually apathetic; too much, and he might well become a snorting bull.

The most pervasive and plentiful of my chemicals is my growth hormone. It played its chief role in Joe's youth, seeing to it that he followed normal growth patterns until his bone ends closed and no further height could be added. But my growth hormone may still have jobs to do for Joe, even though he is 47 years old. If he breaks a bone, it is believed to hasten development of new bone; if he nicks himself with a razor, it is thought to hasten healing. It may well encourage growth of new tissues to replace those that have worn out. If something should happen to make me produce this hormone in excess right now—I am quite capable of doing it—growth would resume in Joe's hands, feet, jaws. A great lantern jaw would sprout; Joe's nose would enlarge into a vast bulb; his hands and feet would grow enormously.

It is possible that my growth hormone may turn out to be one of the answers to the cancer riddle—a heady prospect! Cancer, of course, is simply cells growing too rapidly—under my urging, possibly. I know that if research animals are tested with certain cancer-producing chemicals, they develop the disease with almost 100 percent regularity. But remove their pituitaries and there is no cancer! That seems to tie me to the cancer problem—at least in animals. It seems likely that if something were found to offset my growth hormone—possibly an *anti*hormone—development of a cancer could be brought to a halt.

Another pituitary hormone, found only in animals so far, has fascinating possibilities for disease control. This is lipotropin, a hormone that acts as watchdog on fat deposits in the body. It has the striking capacity to move solid fat to the liver, where it is converted into energy. Thus, if properly harnessed, my lipotropin could well be the answer to that paunch Joe is beginning to grow, helping to dissolve it and keep him youthfully trim.

Since I rest in a bony cradle in the center of Joe's head, I am almost perfectly protected from injury. Yet it can happen, and results can be dramatic. Head injury, for example, could lower my production of vasopressin (the antidiuretic hormone), which

Glands of Internal Secretion

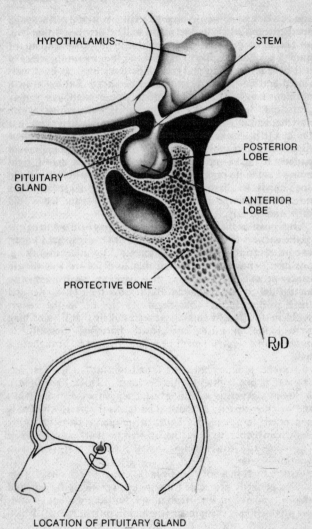

HYPOTHALAMUS

STEM

POSTERIOR LOBE

PITUITARY GLAND

ANTERIOR LOBE

PROTECTIVE BONE

RJD

LOCATION OF PITUITARY GLAND

acts as a brake on the kidneys. The kidneys would go into high gear in producing urine—perhaps gallons of it a day. To survive, of course, Joe would have to drink the same amount of water—something he would have no trouble doing since a constant, raging thirst accompanies this condition.

While injury to me is rare, tumors are less so. And the range of effects of these tumors can be startling. Suppose a tumor should cause me to produce too much of the hormone ACTH, which monitors the hormonal activities of the two adrenal glands sitting astride Joe's kidneys. Joe would develop a great paunch of abdominal fat, and another fat pad would appear on his neck and upper back. His legs would look ridiculously spindly. Blood pressure would soar, sex drive disappear. Calcium would drain from bones; his spinal vertebrae might collapse. Amid all this wreckage, Joe's heart would labor ever harder—and would eventually give up. To forestall this, doctors might decide to try to slow me down with radiation; or they might remove Joe's adrenal glands. Then, of course, Joe would have to be dosed with hormones continually.

Normally, however, I do my work so quietly and so well that Joe can ignore me. Though he can make great contributions to the welfare of his heart, lungs and other organs, he can do nothing for my benefit—except be thankful for me.

THYROID

I AM THAT PINKISH, butterfly-shaped gland that straddles Joe's windpipe just below his Adam's apple. I tip the scales at about two thirds of an ounce. My daily hormone production is less than 1/100,000 ounce. My modest size and productivity would suggest that I am not very important. Actually, I am a powerhouse. I am Joe's thyroid.

Had my hormones been absent at the time of Joe's birth, he would have grown into a thick-lipped, flat-nosed dwarf—an imbecile or moron. My principal job for Joe today, however, is to determine the *rate* at which he lives—whether, metabolically speaking, he creeps like a snail or races like a hare.

You could, I suppose, compare me to a blacksmith's bellows. I fan the fires of life, governing the rate at which Joe's billions of cells burn food into energy. I can either bank the fires or fan them into raging flames. If I were to produce a microscopic pinch too little of my hormones, Joe would probably become puffy-faced, obese, sluggish, dull-witted and, in an extreme case, even a semivegetable. On the other hand, if I were overproductive, he would develop a wolfish appetite but become rail-thin as he burned up his food at a rapid rate. His eyes would pop, maybe so far that the lids couldn't close over them. He would feel jittery, nervous—perhaps a candidate for the psychiatric ward. His heart would race, possibly to a point of exhaustion and death.

Like Joe's other endocrine glands, I am a tiny chemical plant, plucking materials from his bloodstream and fitting them together to make complex hormones. My two main hormones are approximately two thirds iodine. My daily requirements for iodine are roughly only 1/5000 gram—and there are 28 grams in an ounce. Yet this microscopic amount spells the difference between idiocy and healthy development in infancy, the difference between vigor and sickly lassitude in adulthood.

I won't trouble you with all the details of my virtuoso chemistry, but a few highlights might be interesting. Iodine comes to me from Joe's digestive tract in the form of iodide. My enzymes (I have several different ones that perform various tasks) make the conversion into iodine and then hook this iodine to an amino acid within me called tyrosine. After this chemical marriage has taken place, I can then form my two chief hormones. Next, my enzymes step in again to hook molecules of these hormones to Joe's blood proteins so that they can hitchhike to the remotest corners of Joe's body.

The potency of my hormones is striking. A tadpole without thyroid hormone will not become a frog. My hormones stimulate virtually all of the vast multitude of cells in Joe's body.

Because of their power my hormones must be kept under exact control, providing only the energy needed at any given moment. When Joe's wife was pregnant, her thyroid provided slightly more hormones than usual, to help fill her special needs. As Joe sleeps, his energy requirements are minimal. But even the slightest activity steps things up. Simply sitting up in bed boosts his energy needs considerably; standing increases them even more; really heavy exercise lifts them manifold. Heavy mental exercise scarcely raises energy requirements at all. Half a peanut an hour would fill the need while Joe works on his income-tax return.

Two other glands help me maintain the necessary control of my hormone production. The hypothalamus, a nubbin of tissue

Glands of Internal Secretion

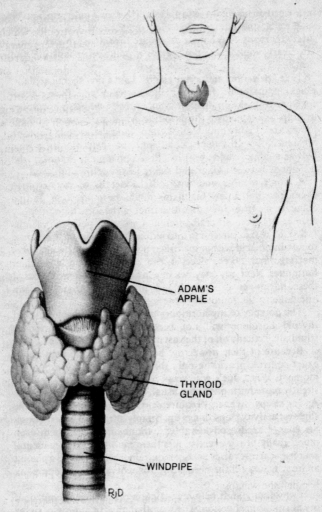

ADAM'S APPLE

THYROID GLAND

WINDPIPE

RJD

in Joe's brain, stimulates the pituitary, up under Joe's brain. The pituitary in turn produces the hormone thyrotropin, which targets on me, telling me to get to work to meet current energy needs. When I produce too much hormone, the excess shuts off the pituitary stimulus. This feedback keeps production on an even keel.

As you see, I am under nervous as well as chemical control. This explains why stress or worry may be capable of causing me to produce excessive amounts of hormone—enough to make a jittery wreck of Joe, enough even to put him in a mental hospital. A death in the family, business failure, a serious auto accident, extensive surgery, marital trouble: pile any of these on top of another over a period of months or years, and a chain reaction gets under way. The worrying brain may cause the hypothalamus to overstimulate the pituitary, which in turn overstimulates me. I start driving Joe at a pace he cannot stand.

In many respects, I am one of the weakest spots in Joe's body. A great deal can go wrong with me. My controls are so precise, my hormone production is so dependent on so many other factors, that failure anywhere along the line can spell trouble.

Lack of iodine is a common cause of trouble. Joe, like most people in developed countries, has little problem here. Seafoods and also vegetables grown in soils near the sea are rich in iodine. If these foods are not available, then the use of iodized salt meets Joe's and my iodine requirement. People elsewhere in the world aren't so fortunate. In mountainous regions, iodine is almost always missing in the soil and water. The same is true in areas once glaciated; as glaciers melted, they washed iodine out of the soil. And in many such places iodized salt is not readily available.

My response to iodine hunger is to grow larger, to add millions of new cells in an effort to capture any iodine available. My weight may shoot up from less than an ounce to several ounces. This is an iodine-deficient goiter—"nontoxic" goiter—which is disturbing as far as looks are concerned but rarely dangerous to health, unless the gland grows large enough to pinch the windpipe.

A variety of things can slow me into relative inactivity. Let a hereditary defect, certain drugs or disease knock out any of my crucial enzymes and my hormone production slows or stops. Also, for reasons not understood, I may simply decide to shut up business, to atrophy or be replaced by nonfunctioning thyroid tissue. Or Joe's pituitary may go on the fritz and produce too little of the stimulating hormone I need.

At the other extreme, many things can send me off on a spree of overproduction—and I may enlarge diffusely just as I do when I'm short of iodine. This time, however, the trouble is known as "toxic" goiter. Strangely enough, excessive iodine can cause this. Or, a tumor may develop in Joe's pituitary, causing it to produce too much thyrotropin, stimulating me to flood his body with hormone.

Cancer is another of my many ills. But the cancer that strikes me is among the better-behaved ones. It tends to remain localized rather than to spread. A surgeon can get at it and remove it, with high hopes of a cure. Or it may be treated with thyroid pills to put the growth to sleep and decrease its size.

Fortunately, doctors know a great deal about taking care of my ills—probably more than about any of Joe's other endocrine glands. If I am going at a laggard pace, they can pep Joe up by supplying missing hormone in pill form. If I am producing hormone too enthusiastically, any one of several drugs can be prescribed that will interfere with my enzymes, and hence with my hormone production. Or, Joe may be asked to swig a cocktail containing radioactive iodine. This, like ordinary iodine, will find its way straight to me, and the radiation will start hammering my overproductive cells into submission. Since radioactive iodine decays rapidly, virtually all radiation ceases within a few weeks.

Most overactive thyroids are treated by the methods described above. However, some patients do require surgery. In the operation, the surgeon must decide the exact amount of me to remove. If he takes too little, I'll continue to produce too much hormone; if he takes too much, supportive therapy with thyroid hormone pills will be required.

How does a doctor know that I am making mischief? If Joe shows finger tremor in an outstretched hand, is nervous and having sleeping problems, has a big appetite but keeps losing weight, any doctor will suspect hyperactivity in me. If Joe is puffy-faced and sluggish, *hypo*activity—underactivity—is suggested.

Tests, of course, can usually aid the good clinician. In one, a blood sample is drawn and the amount of hormone hitchhiking on blood proteins is measured—an excellent test of my activity. About a dozen tests have been developed, and only a doctor can decide which are the best for any patient.

I believe I hold yet-to-be-revealed secrets. Research just discovered the hormone calcitonin in the 1960s, and I can assure you that it has a big future. Calcium is one of the body's major minerals—the main constituent of bones and teeth. The hormone produced by the parathyroid glands, my neighbors and associates, tends to elevate the calcium in Joe's blood, mainly by draining it from his bones. Too much drain and they lose strength. My calcitonin helps to offset this and to keep things in balance.

When more facts are in, calcitonin may prove valuable in preventing the bones of the elderly from becoming brittle and breakable. Since this is out of my jurisdiction, I can't promise, but it is a possibility. In any event, I think I am safe in saying that you haven't heard the last of me.

THYMUS

UNTIL RECENTLY I've been regarded as a kind of poor relation in Joe's family of glands. Like his appendix, I was looked on as an evolutionary leftover—useless, nonproductive, a source of no good and possibly of trouble. How times change! All of a sudden I find myself the hottest item in medical research—the possible key to problems ranging from allergy and arthritis to cancer and aging. I am Joe's thymus gland.

In appearance I am anything but glamorous—an insignificant-looking little blob of yellow-gray tissue, about the size of a matchbook, nestled between Joe's lungs just at the top of his breastbone. (Joe has probably sampled my relatives in a meal. The neck sweetbread from a calf is its thymus.) My size is determined by age. I weigh a third of an ounce now. But I weighed twice that when Joe was born, and six times that when he reached puberty.

In my new role as a glamour organ, I'm being called "the throne of immunity." What is immunity? Basically, it is the body's effort to recognize and destroy any intruder that might be a source of harm—and this includes just about everything: bacteria, viruses, the wrong type of blood, a splinter in the finger, fungi, cancer cells, poisons, transplanted skin, you name it. In a sense, Joe's body is a fortress with troops instantly ready to attack any invader—*anything* that is non-Joe. I am a chief component of Joe's defense force, which is, in its way, more complex than the defense system of any country. I support its many elements—the spleen, lymph nodes, bone marrow, tonsils, adenoids, maybe the appendix and possibly portions of the intestine.

Some idea of my importance is given by the fact that when Joe was in his mother's womb, I was larger than his heart, even larger than a lung. To a great extent Joe came into the world defenseless against disease—except for the immune factors passed from his mother's bloodstream into his. And these would perish in a very short time. Had Joe been born without me—as infants are from time to time—the most trivial infection would have become a threat to life. He would have been a runty, sickly little babe, and within a few months might have died.

Instead, with me, little Joe was soon ready to fight infection on his own. He had in his bone marrow a host of microscopic white cells, immature "seedlings" of cells called lymphocytes. These fledgling warrior cells were passed to me via his bloodstream. It was my task to hurry them toward maturity, and then send them to the spleen, lymphatic system and other organs for final growing up. I also gave these organs hormonal stimulus to prod them into activity. Within days I had little Joe's immunity shaping up. I've been running the system ever since.

These lymphocytes produced by me, and another group possibly produced somewhere in the intestine, are extraordinary performers—part detective, part killer. Representing a fourth of Joe's white blood cells, they instantly recognize any potential enemy—a flu virus, a pus-forming staphylococcus, a thorn that has penetrated a finger. Immediately they sound a general alarm.

Suppose Joe cuts his finger and a minor infection follows. To my lymphocytes, *nothing* is minor. They start pouring out antibodies and call upon other cells to do the same. Each antibody is specific against a single invader—one for mumps,

Glands of Internal Secretion

one for whooping cough and so on. Joe may have as many as a million different kinds. The antibodies attack and slaughter the invading microbes in the cut. Meanwhile, the lymphocytes have joined forces with phagocytes, other white cells in the blood, which simply eat the bacterial debris. Joe's cut finger heals uneventfully. He thinks nothing of the matter, although actually quite a Waterloo has occurred.

Sometimes my lymphocytes overestimate the danger, and respond *too* aggressively, producing a whole array of annoying symptoms. This *over*response to an invader—to ragweed pollen,

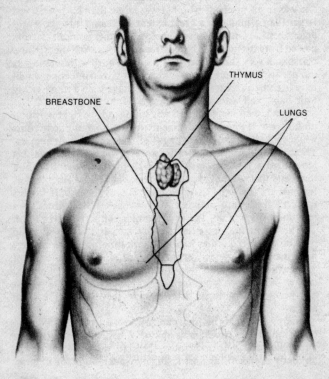

THYMUS

BREASTBONE

LUNGS

for example—is termed an allergy. Like other people, Joe has a few mild allergies and considers them a nuisance. But they at least tell him that his immune system is working.

As I have said, Joe has *two* immune systems. The one with possible headquarters in his intestine is mainly concerned with bacterial and viral invasions. While my lymphocytes are active against some bacteria and viruses, their main enemies are allergens, a wide variety of fungus infections, and foreign tissue. Suppose Joe one day receives a liver transplant. Unless suppressed, my lymphocytes, recognizing the new liver as non-Joe, would start producing antibodies, and the new liver would be rejected. That's why, before transplant surgery, Joe's doctor would treat me and my supportive organs with drugs and radiation to inactivate us. But with us out of the picture even temporarily, transplant patients may die of overwhelming infection.

In later life, the immune response—like everything else—slows down. Is this why older people are more susceptible to cancer than the young? It seems possible. Another point here. Doctors have long been suspicious of "spontaneous" cancer cures—cancers that simply disappear for no known reason. Today these cases are too well documented to doubt. I have two possible explanations for them.

Maybe for some reason the immune system was temporarily out of order. The cancer got a running start. Then the immune system repaired itself, came awake, began a vigorous attack. End of cancer. It may also be that surgical removal of cancerous tissue, even though incomplete, sometimes allows the immune mechanism to reject the remaining tumor when it could not handle the original mass. Some patients, particularly children, may therefore be cured. I cannot swear that these are the explanations for such baffling cases. But it seems reasonable.

Nothing as complex as my immune system can be expected to function perfectly all the time. My lymphocytes sometimes bungle, mistaking normal body tissue as foreign stuff to be attacked. They may attack linings of joints, causing painful inflammation—rheumatoid arthritis. If a means could be found to teach my haywire lymphocytes to behave, we might see the end of the most common form of arthritis.

Glands of Internal Secretion

In Joe, as in other humans, I am particularly hit by stress. Stress of any kind is a deadly wrecker of internal organs—whether it be sustained noise, fear, fatigue or disease. I am one of its chief victims. If the stress is severe enough, I may shrink to a third of my normal size in the course of a few days. Clearly, I must play some important role in combating stress, but what that role is I do not know.

I no longer seem to be as essential to Joe as I once was, now that he's grown up. My production of lymphocytes is no longer of critical importance, since the ones that I distributed to other organs long ago are now firmly rooted and in full production. Just the same, if I were destroyed by a tumor, Joe might be hit by a whole bookful of misery: fungi might start chewing up fingernails, painful fungus infection of the mouth develops, muscles become inflamed and weak—and enough other afflictions to make life hardly worth living. So the whole story of my essentiality in later life still isn't in.

This is certainly true of my recently discovered hormone, thymosin. Once I have emptied it into Joe's bloodstream, it has a stimulating effect on the entire immunity system, pepping up the spleen, prodding the lymphatic system to produce lymphocytes in adequate numbers. If Joe ever got a severe dose of radiation—enough to knock out his immune system—my hormone might be a lifesaver, stimulating the spleen and other organs that had shut down to get back into production. One curious thing about my hormone: as Joe gets older, I taper off production, and will shut down entirely when he reaches about 50. Is this an important part of the aging process, and might shots of thymosin slow it? I don't know.

To a great degree, I'm still the big question mark of Joe's body. My story is still being unraveled. Naturally, I'm flattered by all the attention I'm getting. All I can say is, it's about time! All along I've known my importance. I'm surprised it took others so long to discover it.

ADRENAL

GRAM FOR GRAM, I pack more dynamite than any other organ in Joe's body. I can cripple him, sicken him, send him to the madhouse, kill him. I haven't done any of these things, of course. In fact, I have behaved so well that Joe is barely aware of my existence.

I am the adrenal gland that perches on top of his right kidney. Like a little jockey, my twin partner rides the other. I am roughly the shape of a tricorne hat, not much larger than the tip of a finger; I weigh about as much as a nickel. But my talents are immense: it would take acres of chemical plant to synthesize the 50-odd hormones or hormonelike substances that I manufacture. Although I produce less than a thousandth of an ounce of them a day, they play key roles in just about everything Joe does.

I am absolutely essential to life. Remove my partner and me, and Joe would be dead in a day or so—unless his doctor started feeding him artificial hormones in a hurry. Slow down our work, and watch Joe's life slow down, too. Soon he would become weak, debilitated—a mere shell of his former self.

Had a portion of me become overactive when Joe was a boy,

the results would have been similarly striking. The little lad would have become a little man. His voice would have deepened, his beard sprouted, his sexual apparatus taken on manly proportions. Bone ends, which should remain open and soft until full growth is reached, would have closed prematurely. And Joe would have gone through life as a runty fellow.

For a long time I was the mystery organ of Joe's body. No one knew what I did—only that my removal meant death. As chemists began to pry out my secrets, they discovered my virtuosity. When they learned of my cortisonelike hormones, for instance, they were truly astonished—for these substances alone are useful in treating upward of 100 diseases, ranging from gout to ulcerative colitis to asthma.

And consider my architecture. I have one of the richest networks of blood vessels found in the body. Each minute, six times my weight of blood passes through me. I also have a big reserve capacity. Ten percent of my tissue is sufficient to meet Joe's normal needs for my hormones. However, if I were to dwindle down to the ten-percent level, and Joe faced a really big stress—a severe illness, say, or major surgery—it would very likely kill him. He wouldn't have enough of my protective hormones to save him.

Actually, I produce two basic sets of hormones. My medulla, or core, makes one set; my cortex, or rind, the other. My core has a unique feature: its own hot line to Joe's brain. Let Joe have any strong emotion—a sudden rage, an overwhelming fear—and my medulla gets the information instantly. Obviously, I don't know the nature of the emergency. So I prepare Joe for either fight *or* flight. My medulla starts pouring two hormones—adrenalin and noradrenalin—into Joe's bloodstream.

The response of Joe's body is extraordinary. His liver immediately releases stored sugar—instant energy—into his bloodstream. My hormones shut down skin blood vessels—Joe goes pale—and start sluicing this extra blood into muscles and internal organs. Joe's heart speeds up, and arteries tighten to hoist blood pressure. Digestion comes to a halt—no time to worry about that detail right now—and the clotting time of Joe's blood is quickened, in case of injury.

I've accomplished all this in seconds. Suddenly, Joe is a

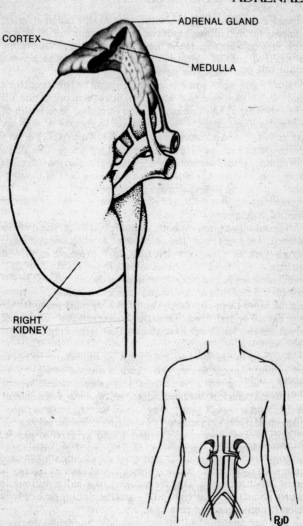

ADRENAL GLAND

CORTEX

MEDULLA

RIGHT
KIDNEY

RJD

71

virtual superman. If his survival necessitates running faster, jumping farther, hitting harder or lifting more than ever before, he is now capable of it. He has heard stories of individuals lifting overturned cars to release trapped victims. It was *adrenal* hormones that made this possible.

Obviously, such stimulation can't go on indefinitely; Joe's body would race itself to death. So, a tricky bit of protection has gone to work. The same stresses that stimulate production of adrenalin also cause the hypothalamus to signal the pituitary gland to release a substance called ACTH. This ACTH in turn prods my cortex, or rind, into stepping up production of *its* hormones. Under conditions of stress, it's the job of these hormones to maintain blood pressure and the flow of blood to vital organs, and to help convert fat and protein into sugar—an immediately utilizable form of energy. Soon, everything is under control once again.

The hormones that my cortex produces fall into three broad classes. One set (of the cortisone family) superintends metabolism of fats, carbohydrates and proteins; a second watches over water and mineral balance in Joe's body. The third batch is the sex hormones, supplementing those produced by the gonads. Since these hormones can't be stored, I must manufacture them constantly, and the liver must see to it that any excess is destroyed. Thus the hormones that my cortex produced two hours ago have already been largely replaced by a fresh supply.

Keeping things in exact balance is all-important. Suppose something happens to Joe—an injury, a disease—that knocks out the working cells of my cortex. Until research men learned how to manufacture my chief hormones, this was a sentence of death. And it wasn't pretty. The victim seemed to get a dozen diseases at once. Skin took on a bronze tint; anemia developed; muscles wasted away; weight and blood pressure dropped; appetite dwindled; there was nausea, vomiting, diarrhea. Steadily, the victim grew weaker and weaker, and death was usually welcome. Fortunately, Joe doesn't have to worry about this today; should anything happen to my cortex, artificial hormones could allow him to lead a near-normal life.

Too much of my cortical hormones can be almost as bad as

too little. Suppose there is too much cortisol—my hormone of the cortisone family. Joe's arms and legs would shrivel as the excess converted muscle protein into sugar. Drained of minerals, bones would become brittle. Fat would accumulate across Joe's back and in folds on his abdomen, overloading his now spindly legs. Blood pressure would soar; mental aberrations would become common.

Another of the major hormones of my cortex is aldosterone, which helps maintain a mineral and water balance in Joe's body. Too much—even by a pinhead amount—and Joe would be in real trouble. Vital potassium would be lost in urine, and excess sodium (salt) would be retained. Joe's muscles would weaken and possibly become paralyzed. His heart would race, his blood pressure soar, his fingers tingle; headache would be continuous and almost unbearable. Aldosterone overproduction is usually caused by tumors, and when the tumor is removed, recovery is assured.

Obviously, none of these things has happened to Joe; not yet, anyway. They merely indicate what a Pandora's box I *can* be. For years now, I have done my many jobs so well that Joe has almost forgotten I exist. He'd better not forget completely, though, because there is something he can do to help ensure my continued well-being.

Joe should remember that too much stress—too much worry, anger, hate—is bad for him *and* for me. Thus he might try to calm down a bit.

5

Circulatory System

HEART

I'M CERTAINLY no beauty. I weigh 12 ounces, am red-brown in color and have an unimpressive shape. I am the dedicated slave of Joe. I am Joe's heart.

I hang by ligaments in the center of his chest. I am about six inches long and, at my widest point, four inches across—more pear-shaped than valentine. Whatever you may have heard about me from poets, I am really not a very romantic character. I am just a hardworking four-chambered pump—actually *two* pumps, one to move blood to the lungs, the other to push it out into the body. Every day, I would say, I pump blood through 60,000 miles of blood vessels. That's enough pumping to fill a 4000-gallon tank car.

When Joe thinks of me at all, he thinks of me as fragile and delicate. Delicate! When so far in his life I have pumped more than 300,000 *tons* of blood? I work twice as hard as the leg muscles of a dash runner, or the arm muscles of a heavyweight boxing champ. Let them try to go at my pace and they would turn to jelly in minutes. No muscles in the body are as strong as I am—except those of a woman's uterus as she expels a baby. But uterine muscles don't keep at it day and night for 70 years, as I am expected to do.

That, of course, is a slight exaggeration. I do rest—between beats. It takes about three tenths of a second for my big left ventricle to contract and push blood out into the body. Then I have a rest period of half a second. Also, while Joe sleeps, a large percentage of his capillaries are inactive; this means that I don't have to push blood through them, and my beat slows from a normal 72 down to 55.

Joe almost never thinks of me—which is good. I don't want him to become one of those heart neurotics and worry us *both* into real trouble. When he does worry about me it is almost always about the wrong things. One night, as he was drifting off to sleep, Joe was listening to my quiet thumping—that's the opening and closing of my valves—and he thought he heard me "skip" a beat. He was quite worried. Was I giving out on him? He needn't have been concerned.

From time to time, my ignition system gets momentarily out of whack—just like the ignition system on Joe's car. I generate my own electricity, and send out impulses to trigger contraction. But occasionally I will misfire, piling one beat on top of another. It sounds as if I have "skipped"—but I haven't. Joe would be surprised how often this happens when he isn't listening.

After a nightmare he sometimes wakes up and worries because I am racing. That's because when he runs for his life in his dreams, I run too. Joe's worries actually aggravate things—make me go still faster. If he would calm down, so would I. But if he can't, there is a way to slow me down. The vagus nerves act as a brake. They pass up through the neck—behind the ears, at the hinge of the jaw. Gentle massage here will slow my beat.

Joe blames almost everything on me—fatigue, dizzy spells and such. But I have little to do with his fatigue, and his occasional dizzy spells usually trace to his ears. From time to time he will be doing desk work, and will get a sharp pain in the chest. He fears that he is about to have a heart attack. He needn't worry. That pain comes from his digestive tract—payment for the heavy meal eaten a couple of hours earlier. When *I* am in trouble, I usually send out a pain signal only after undue exertion or emotion. That's the way I tell him I am not getting enough nourishment to carry the work he is loading on me.

How do I get my nourishment? From the blood, of course. But, although I represent only 1/200 of the body weight, I require about 1/20 of the blood supply. That means I consume about ten times the nourishment required by the body's other organs and tissues.

But I don't extract nourishment from the blood passing through my four chambers. I am fed by my own two coronary

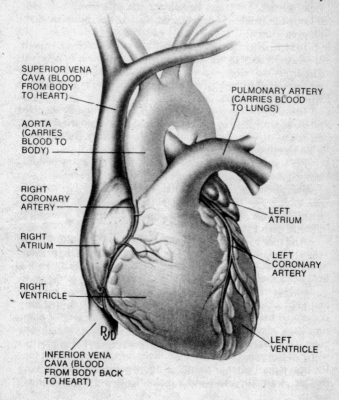

SUPERIOR VENA CAVA (BLOOD FROM BODY TO HEART)

PULMONARY ARTERY (CARRIES BLOOD TO LUNGS)

AORTA (CARRIES BLOOD TO BODY)

RIGHT CORONARY ARTERY

LEFT ATRIUM

RIGHT ATRIUM

LEFT CORONARY ARTERY

RIGHT VENTRICLE

LEFT VENTRICLE

INFERIOR VENA CAVA (BLOOD FROM BODY BACK TO HEART)

arteries—little branching "trees" with trunks not much larger than soda straws. This is my weak spot. Trouble here is the greatest single cause of death.

No one knows how it happens, but early in life—sometimes even at birth in the hearts of some Joes—fatty deposits begin to build up in the coronary arteries. Gradually, they can close an artery. Or, a clot may form to close it suddenly.

When an artery shuts down, the portion of the heart muscle it feeds dies. This leaves scar tissue—perhaps it is no larger than a small marble, but it can be half the size of a tennis ball. How serious the trouble is depends on the size and position of the plugged artery.

Joe had a heart attack five years ago and didn't even know it. He was too busy to notice that tiny twinge of pain in his chest. The artery that clogged was a small one on my rear wall. It took me two weeks to sweep away the dead tissue and repave the area with a scar not much larger than a pea.

Joe comes from a family where heart disease has occurred often, so statistics say that I am going to give him trouble, too. Of course, he can't do anything about his heredity. But he can do a lot to minimize the risk.

Let's start with overweight. Joe is getting extra padding around the middle and jokes about his middle-age spread. It's no laughing matter. Every pound of his excess fat contains something like 200 *miles* of capillaries which I have to push blood through. And that is in addition to the work of carrying around each extra pound.

And that brings me to Joe's blood pressure. It's 140/90—the upper limit of normal for his age. The 140 measures the pressure I work against while contracting, and the 90 is the pressure while I am resting between beats. The lower figure is the more important. The higher that figure rises, the less rest I get. And without adequate rest a heart simply works itself to death.

There are a lot of things Joe could do to get his blood pressure down to safer levels. The first is to get rid of excess poundage. He would be surprised at the drop in blood pressure that would follow.

Smoking is another thing. Joe smokes two packs a day—which means he may be absorbing 80 to 120 milligrams of nicotine every 24 hours. This is pretty violent stuff. It constricts arteries, particularly in the hands and feet, which raises the pressure against which I must work. It also stimulates *me* so that I beat more rapidly; a cigarette pushes my beat up from a normal 72 into the 80s. Joe tells himself that it is too late to give up smoking—that the damage is done. But, if he could get rid of that constant nicotine stimulation, things would be easier for me.

Joe could give me a break in other ways. He is a competitive, driving, worrying sort of fellow—you know, the successful-businessman type. He doesn't realize that his constant fretting continually stimulates his adrenal glands to produce more adrenalin and noradrenalin. It's the same old story as with nicotine: tightened arteries, higher blood pressure, a faster pace for me.

The point is this: If Joe relaxes, *I* relax. After all, he doesn't have to be going to a fire all the time. An occasional nap would help. And he might try some light reading instead of that stuff he brings home from the office in his briefcase.

Exercise is another thing. Joe is one of those weekend athletes who take it in big doses. He still likes that rushing-up-to-the-net bit in tennis, as if he were a college boy. When he does this, my work load goes up as high as five times normal.

What Joe *should* be doing is taking regular, mild exercise. A walk of a mile or two a day would help. Climbing a couple of flights of stairs to his office wouldn't hurt either. His office is on the tenth floor, but he could walk up the first two flights and then catch the elevator. Little things like that would do a lot. As I said, fatty deposits are already beginning to block some of my arteries. This *regular* exercise causes new blood pathways to develop. Then if one artery closes down there are others to nourish me.

Finally, there is diet. I am not asking Joe to become a diet nut. Just the same, fat *seems* to play some role in building up that plaque forming in my arteries. Joe gets 45 percent of his calories from fats and, like others in industrialized countries who eat this way, he has a 50-50 chance of dying from clogged arteries.

Circulatory System

I wish he could see what happens after a heavy fat meal. Tiny fat globules in the blood seem to glue red blood cells together into a sludgy mess. This is the stuff I must push through capillaries. It's quite a job.

I'm not the demanding type. I'll do the best I can for Joe under *any* circumstances. Just the same, there are those breaks he could give me: slim down a bit, take regular exercise, relax a little more, cut down on fats and smoking. If he would only do those things, I could keep on working for Joe for a long time.

LUNG

I AM JOE'S right lung, and I claim the privilege of speaking since I am slightly larger than my partner in the left side of his chest. I have three lobes—sections—while the left has only two. Joe would be surprised if he could see me. He thinks of me as a kind of hollow, pink football bladder hanging in his chest. I'm not much like that at all. I am not hollow—if you cut through me, I would look something like a rubber bath sponge. And I am not pink. I was when Joe was a baby. Now, a quarter of a million cigarettes plus half a billion breaths of dirty city air later, I am an unattractive slate-gray with a mottling of black.

There are three separate, sealed compartments in Joe's chest: one for me, one for the left lung, one for his heart. I hang loose in my compartment, filling it completely, and weigh a little over a pound.

I have no muscles and hence play a passive role in breathing. There is a slight vacuum in my compartment—so when Joe's chest expands, I expand. When Joe exhales, I collapse. It is simply a recoil mechanism. Let Joe puncture his chest wall in an accident and my vacuum is broken. I'll hang loose, doing no work, until healing takes place and the vacuum is re-established.

Take a closer look at my architecture. Joe's four-inch-long windpipe divides at its lower end into two main bronchial tubes—one for me, one for my partner. Then branching begins in me—like an upside-down tree. First the larger bronchi, then the bronchioles 1/100 of an inch in diameter. These are simply air passages. My real work is done in my alveoli—grapelike bunches of minute air sacs. Flattened out, their tissue would probably cover half a tennis court.

Each alveolus is covered with a cobweb of capillaries. Blood is pumped by the heart into one end of a capillary. Red cells pass through single-file—the passage taking about a second—and a remarkable thing takes place. Through the gossamer membrane of the capillary wall, the cells diffuse their cargo of carbon dioxide into my alveoli. At the same time, the cells pick up oxygen going the other way. It's a kind of gaseous swap shop—blue blood flowing in one end of the capillary, emerging refreshed and cherry-red at the other.

Joe's more important body organs—notably the heart—are under automatic control. Most of the time this is true of me, too, though I am under voluntary control as well. As a child, Joe had temper tantrums and would sometimes hold his breath until he turned a faint blue. His mother worried, unnecessarily. Long before he got into any real trouble, automatic respiration would take over. He would start breathing whether he wanted to or not.

My automatic breathing control is in the medulla oblongata—the bulge where the spinal cord taps into the brain. It's an amazingly sensitive chemical detector. Laboring muscles burn oxygen rapidly and pour out waste carbon dioxide. As it accumulates, the blood becomes slightly acid. The respiratory control center detects this instantly and orders me to work faster. Let the levels rise high enough, as when Joe does heavy exercise, and it orders *deeper* breathing as well—one's "second wind."

Lying quietly in bed, Joe needs about eight quarts of air a minute. Sitting up requires 16; walking, 24; running, 50. Since Joe is a desk worker, he has no large oxygen demands.

Normally, he breathes about 16 times a minute—a pint of air each time. (This only partially inflates me. I can hold eight times as much.) Even so, not all of that one-pint breath reaches me; one third of it shuffles aimlessly in and out of the windpipe and other air passages.

I like my air just about as moist and warm as that in a tropical swamp. Producing this very special air in the space of a few inches is quite a trick. The same tear glands that bathe Joe's eyes, plus other moisture-secreting glands in his nose and throat, produce as much as a pint of fluid a day to humidify my air. Surface blood vessels along the same route—wide open on cold days, closed on warm days—take care of the heating job.

There is an almost endless list of things that can cause me trouble. Each day, Joe breathes in a variety of bacteria and viruses. Lysozyme in the nose and throat, a powerful microbe slayer, destroys most of these. And those that slip into my dark, warm, moist passages—a microbial happy hunting ground—I can usually handle. Phagocytes patrol my passages and simply wrap themselves around invaders and eat them.

Dirty air, of course, is my biggest challenge. Other organs lead sheltered, protected lives, but for all practical purposes I am *outside* Joe's body—exposed to environmental hazards and contaminants. I am really quite delicate, and it's a wonder I am able to survive at all, having to deal with such things as sulfur dioxide, benzopyrene, lead, nitrogen dioxide. Since some of them actually melt nylon stockings, you can guess what they do to me.

My air-cleaning process—such as it is—begins with hairs in the nose, which trap large dust particles. Sticky mucus in nose, throat and bronchial passages acts as flypaper to trap finer particles. But the real cleaning job falls to the cilia. These are microscopic hairs—tens of millions of them—along my air passages. They wave back and forth, like wheat in the wind, about 12 times a second. Their upward thrust sweeps mucus from lower passages to the throat, where it can be swallowed.

If Joe could watch my cilia under a microscope, he'd see that if cigarette smoke or badly contaminated air is blown on them, the wind-in-the-wheatfield action stops. A temporary paralysis sets in. Let this irritation continue long enough, and the cilia

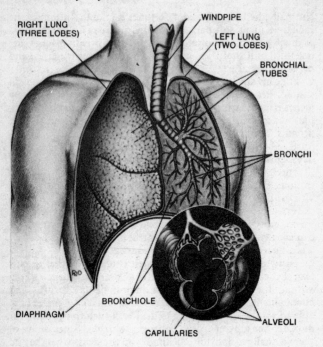

RIGHT LUNG
(THREE LOBES)

WINDPIPE

LEFT LUNG
(TWO LOBES)

BRONCHIAL
TUBES

BRONCHI

BRONCHIOLE

DIAPHRAGM

CAPILLARIES

ALVEOLI

wither and die, never to be replaced.

After 30 years of smoking, Joe has lost most of his cilia, and mucus-secreting membranes in his air passages have thickened to three times normal size. Joe doesn't know it, but he is in actual danger of drowning. If enough mucus drops down into my air sacs, it halts breathing just as effectively as a lungful of water. One thing saves Joe from this: his noisy, inefficient smoker's cough, which has replaced the quiet efficiency of the cilia. Joe might remember that it's the only cleaning method left to me—and be cautious about taking cough-suppressing drugs.

A large part of the time, Joe is asking me to breathe real garbage. Some of the particles clog my smaller passages, and some actually scar my tissues. The fragile walls of my alveoli lose elasticity. They don't collapse the way they should when I exhale. (Thus it is possible to breathe *in* but not *out*.) Carbon dioxide is trapped in them, and they can no longer contribute oxygen to the blood or extract waste carbon dioxide. The result is emphysema—a fearsome trial in which each breath represents a fight for survival.

Although Joe doesn't know it, this has already happened to a few million of my alveoli. Since Joe has about eight times the lung capacity he needs for desk work, he still has plenty of reserve. But lately he has noticed that even a small amount of exertion brings on breathlessness. I'm warning him.

Joe should heed the old medical saying, "If you are aware that you have lungs, you are already in trouble," and take a little better care of me. In the main, this means giving me better air to breathe. The big thing, of course, would be to give up smoking. Short of this, there are other things he can do. There is a small, reasonably priced machine which circulates room air through a thin bed of activated carbon—the stuff used in gas masks—and cleanses this air of chemicals deadly to my tissues. One in Joe's bedroom would give me some eight hours of protection, and another in his office would provide eight more.

A little more exercise and more sensible eating would be in order. Any general body exercise—climbing stairs, walking, jogging, sports—forces me to breathe more deeply, which is all to the good. And there are exercises for me alone. Ordinarily, the best breathing is deep breathing—more air at a slower pace. Joe could practice abdominal breathing, the way babies and opera singers do: not by inflating the manly chest, but by dropping the diaphragm down. Then air is sucked into even my deepest alveoli.

Joe could also give me a housecleaning a few times each day. He thinks that with a normal exhalation I'm empty. By no means. Let him blow out all the air he can via his mouth. Then if he will purse his lips, he can do quite a lot more blowing. If he does this while smoking, he will see something that should give him pause: smoke trailing out through his pursed lips that would normally be left in me to stagnate.

It all adds up to this: Most of my neighbor organs can absorb an enormous amount of abuse without complaint. I can't. Nature hasn't equipped me with all the defenses I really need in today's world. That's why a variety of lung diseases have reached epidemic proportions.

Boss Joe, take heed!

BLOODSTREAM

THINK BIG when you think about me. I am a transport system with 75,000 miles of route—more than a global airline. I am also a garbage man and delivery boy with 60 *trillion* customers—that's 17,000 times the number of people there are on earth. My customers are the cells in Joe's body. I haul away their wastes and provide them with the essentials of life. I am Joe's bloodstream.

He thinks of me as a sluggish river, and is hardly aware of the frenzied activity under way within me at all times. In the second it takes Joe to blink his eyelids, 1.2 *million* of my red cells reach the end of their 120-day life span and perish. In that same second, Joe's marrow, mostly in his ribs, skull and vertebrae, produces an equal number of new cells. In a lifetime these bones will manufacture about half a *ton* of red cells. During its short life, each red cell will make something like 75,000 round trips from Joe's heart to other parts of his body.

How do I get around Joe's body? Joe's heart is my main pump—and not a very good one as far as I am concerned. It pumps in surges, and it is therefore up to my big arteries to even the irregular flow, expanding with the pumping stroke, contracting between beats, so that blood arrives as a steady stream in my extremities. By the time the blood is ready to return to the heart through my veins, pressure has dropped to near zero. Left on its own, the blood would never get back.

Yet I keep it moving—from toes back to heart—aided by muscles outside my system. An awkward arrangement, but it works. As Joe's leg muscles contract, they squeeze veins and push blood upward (regularly spaced valves prevent backflow). That's why walking is an excellent stimulator of circulation. (If the valves leak, the veins are apt to stretch and become clogged with clotted blood. That's a varicose vein—often painful, always troublesome.)

Basically, the fluid that flows through my intricate pipeline system consists of red cells, a bewildering array of leucocytes, or white blood cells—granulocytes, lymphocytes, monocytes—as well as platelets and a variety of other, soluble constituents such as cholesterol, sugar, salts, enzymes and fats, plus liquid plasma to float everything in. To assure safe blood volume and pressure, my liquidity must always be maintained at the proper level. To be on the safe side, I absorb virtually all the water that Joe drinks—excreting any excess via urine, sweat and exhaled air. When water is in short supply, I conserve every drop and cry for help. That's why the badly wounded always beg for water.

Everyone is familiar with my basic blood groups—O, A, B and AB. But my blood also contains a great variety of other factors (M, N. P, Rh, etc.), and new ones are identified all the time. There is a growing probability that Joe's blood may be quite as distinctive as his fingerprints, different from all other bloods on earth. In fact, it might be possible to take a blood sample from each person in a large stadium right now, and then a year from now take another sample and assign each fan his proper seat—on the basis of individual blood characteristics.

To distribute oxygen and food to cells, I operate like a municipal water-supply system. The heart pumps, blood is pushed through arteries that grow ever smaller, and finally the flow gets to the capillaries. These gossamer cobwebs, which link arteries and veins, are where the *real* action takes place.

Capillaries are so small that red blood cells must squeeze

through in single file, occasionally even twisting themselves into odd shapes to make it. But in the second or so required for passage there is a whirlwind of activity. It's like unloading a delivery truck, then reloading it with items no longer wanted. The big thing to be unloaded, of course, is oxygen, and carbon dioxide from cellular combustion is the main waste product reloaded in its place.

But the variety of other merchandise delivered to the tissues is amazing. The shopping lists of individual tissue and organ

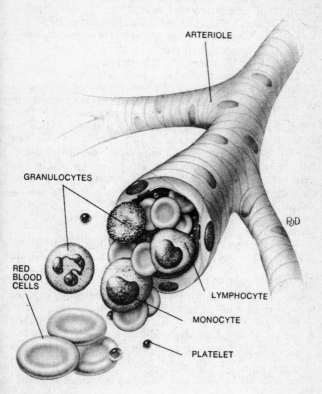

ARTERIOLE

GRANULOCYTES

RED
BLOOD
CELLS

LYMPHOCYTE

MONOCYTE

PLATELET

cells are by no means the same. One cell will want a smidgen of cobalt; others will call for minerals, vitamins, hormones, glucose, fats, amino acids or a simple drink of water. If Joe is exercising, tissue requirements for just about everything increase enormously. His skin will flush—indicating that capillaries are operating at full capacity. When he sleeps, cellular food requirements become minimal and over 90 percent of his capillaries close down.

In the final analysis, Joe is only as healthy as his capillaries. He thinks he breathes with his lungs, eats with his mouth, absorbs food from his intestine. Actually, he does these things in his capillaries. That's why his physician always takes a hard look with an ophthalmoscope at the retinas of Joe's eyes—about the only place in the body where capillaries are clearly visible. If they are clogged and distended, Joe is in trouble.

To keep Joe *out* of trouble, I am constantly alert for any deviation from normal. If I detect a blood loss—whether from a minor cut or a gunshot wound—I immediately rush platelets to the breach. Within seconds they make a temporary patch. Then I start moving up heavier defenses. Fibrin is an essential wound sealer. It isn't normally present in my blood, for it would spell disaster, clogging arteries and bringing almost instant death. But I keep the essential raw material for fibrin's production on hand at all times, and I also carry the enzymes necessary for the chemical conversion that produces it. I can start the process within seconds. After the emergency situation has thus been met, I can take my time about bringing up the raw materials for a permanent seal.

While any break in my pipeline system is a grave emergency, intruders—flu virus, pollen, splinters (the list is endless)—are even greater threats. I have weapons, called antibodies, against upward of a million of these invaders—each designed to attack *just one* individual enemy. It's like having a million-man police force, with each officer specializing in one particular crime.

Perhaps the most striking feature of my antibodies is their memory. Although Joe doesn't recall the mumps he had when he was six—41 years ago—my mumps antibodies do. Let particles of mumps virus slip into his body, and these antibodies will go after them like terriers after a rat. Joe is unaware of the battle, but it is a fight to the death for both combatants. Once they have perished, certain white cells (phagocytes) come along to eat both. I am a tidy housekeeper and don't like dead bodies cluttering up my premises.

In the time you take to read this sentence, I will have received *billions* of replacement antibodies. If it were not for the protection they afford, even the most minor infections could be deadly for Joe.

Since my requirements are so exact, it is little wonder that I am prey to a host of ills. My arteries may harden with calcium infiltration to become as hard as clay pipestems. Fatty deposits collect. These stopped-up, or occluded, arteries can then cause everything from gangrenous toes to stroke or fatal heart attack. Let my sugar (glucose) content rise too high and Joe has diabetes. Let it fall too low and he has hypoglycemia—with palpitation, pallor, sweating, dizziness, weakness. Too few or defective red cells result in anemia.

My white-cell count can drop dramatically in a condition called agranulocytosis. Death may follow in a few days if antibiotics don't prevent infection until recovery occurs. Or, there may be too many white cells—counts rising from a normal 6000 to 8000 per cubic millimeter of blood to 100,000 or more. This is what happens in leukemia. Then too, if my clotting mechanisms are awry, hemophilia or purpura or other bleeding disorders can result.

Can Joe do anything to ease my burdens? A great deal. He can watch his blood pressure—when it is too high, I am under constant stress. Medication can take care of this, keeping pressure at safe levels. Exercise is an *absolute* essential to keep my blood moving properly. Diet is another matter. Too much fat is a proven life-shortener.

In sum, I require far more care than other tissues or organs. But I am worth it, since the health of all those other organs—and hence of Joe himself—largely depends on me.

6
Digestive System

EYETOOTH

I SUPPOSE YOU COULD call me one of the blue-collar
workers of Joe's body. I am not a brilliant chemist
like his liver, or a dedicated slave like his heart. I am the most
perishable part of his body while he lives and, if I survive him,
the most durable after death. It's quite possible that I will be
around several thousand years after the rest of Joe is dust.

I am Joe's upper right canine, or "eye," tooth. With my
twin, the left upper canine and our two opposite numbers in the
lower jaw, I am part of a team that totaled 32 when he began his
adult life. When Joe eats, we teeth start up his digestive process
and contribute to his enjoyment of eating—food wouldn't taste
like much swallowed whole.

Some of our attributes are rather striking. We have one bite
for soft foods, another for hard, and a sensing device that tells us
which to use. We can withstand pressures that would make jelly
of other organs. Kidneys, skin and most of the components of
Joe's body can do some self-repairs when injured. We can't.
Injure us and we stay injured.

My right to speak for the other teeth in Joe's mouth? I think, perhaps, the eyetooth is the most interesting. In Joe's superstitious past, he thought that my roots were so long that they reached to his eye. He was afraid that if I were pulled out, his eye would become diseased. Even though Joe now knows this is nonsense, he still says he would give his eyeteeth for something he wants badly.

We teeth may have started out as scales on fish in ancient seas. But gradually, as life on land began, we changed form and position and became teeth. At birth, Joe had quite a mouthful of us, 52, buried in his gums. We weren't fully formed, but the maturing of 20 "baby" teeth was well under way, including enamel coating. When Joe was newborn, his jaw was small and poorly developed, his face modeled for nursing, not chewing. There was barely room for the baby teeth, and not nearly enough for an adult set of 32.

The gum was our womb. At six months the first of us, the two lower central incisors—Joe calls them his front teeth—began to push their way upward. My baby version came along at 18 months and the second molars, the last baby teeth, at 24 months.

The first permanent teeth—the six-year molars—made their appearance back of all Joe's baby teeth. These molars allowed Joe to chew while his body absorbed the roots of his baby teeth, causing them to loosen and make way for other permanent teeth. I came along when Joe was 12. The last, the wisdom teeth, didn't appear until he was 18.

Look at my structure. I'm quite a piece of engineering. My part that protrudes from the gum has a "skin" of enamel. Although it contains some organic—living—material, it is mainly calcium phosphate. My enamel consists of tiny hexagonal rods, something like bundles of pencils standing on end. It would take 100 of them to bulk as large as a hair. Since my enamel contains no nerves, it is insensitive to pain and is tough enough to stand the ferocious pressures of chewing.

Under my enamel comes the dentine, which is related to bone. Tooth sensitivity begins here. Under the dentine lies my heartland, the pulp, a relatively soft material containing nerves, blood vessels and cells that radiate into the minute tubules of the dentine. The whole tooth structure sits in a tailor-made socket in the jaw, anchored by cementum, a bony tissue, and thousands of fibers. Instead of being an integral part of Joe's jawbone, we are more like plants growing in a flowerpot, rooted according to our jobs. A single root is enough for the cutters up front and me (a tearer of meat and tough food). The heavy-duty grinders farther back may need as many as three for support.

It's no news to Joe that teeth cause trouble! He has already lost four of us, and more are threatened. (Some Joes have lost ten by the age of 40.) Had he cared for us properly this wouldn't have happened. Joe brushes regularly and uses mouthwashes. He *thinks* his mouth is clean. Actually, it is a massive zoo of microbes, and there is little he can do to eliminate them.

For much of his life Joe's great enemy was decay, caused by interaction between bacteria and food particles in the mouth. Debris collects in the crevices on teeth. Joe's dentist calls this plaque, and usually it's invisible. Living bacteria in plaque ferment foods, producing acid. In its turn, the acid dissolves enamel, allowing bacteria to invade the inner structure.

There is another mode of entrance. The enamel in Joe's teeth may have minute fissures that bacteria can slip into and start the decay process *under* the enamel. X rays can spot this hidden decay.

The decay rate slows after age 35. The big thing for Joe to watch for now is periodontal disease, which strikes below the gum line. Here again, plaque is the major culprit. In time, invisible plaque picks up minerals from the saliva to become tartar—which is hard and jagged. Either tartar or plaque can wedge the gum away from the teeth, providing little pockets where food and bacteria lodge. All sorts of misery can result. Gums can become inflamed and bleed. Or bacteria can attack the softer part of the tooth normally protected by gum. Let this continue and pus pockets will form, destroying our attachment to the jaw. At this point it's very likely good-by for us. At his age, most of Joe's serious tooth troubles trace to this process.

If Joe's parents had had his teeth straightened when he was a boy, he wouldn't have had malocclusion, another cause of periodontal disease. Malocclusion means that one of us in the upper jaw doesn't mesh properly with our opposite number below. Thus one tooth works while the other one idles and gets no stimulation in its root area. The gum around the idle one falls

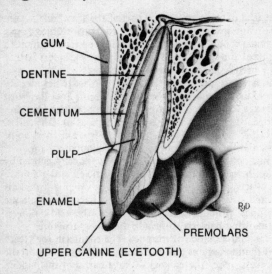

GUM

DENTINE

CEMENTUM

PULP

ENAMEL

PREMOLARS

UPPER CANINE (EYETOOTH)

away, bacteria invade, pus pockets form and the loosening process begins.

I wish people would realize that nowadays both decay and periodontal disease are almost totally preventable. Fluoridated drinking water when Joe was growing up would have made us teeth harder, more resistant to decay. Even at 47, Joe can do a great deal toward minimizing future troubles. Careful brushing and careful cleaning between teeth are essential. The toothpick may be socially taboo but it's a great cleaner. So is dental floss, and the new water jets are fine. It's a good idea to clean after a meal, and particularly after a sweet dessert. This clears away sugar that bacteria thrive on.

Joe's dentist can show him how to find his enemy, the invisible plaque that superficial brushing leaves mostly untouched. It takes only a few minutes every day. Joe simply chews a special tablet containing food coloring which is available at drugstores. The plaque will show up in red patches and he can brush it away before it harms us.

100

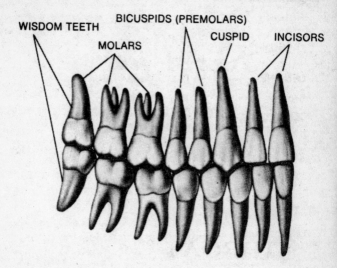

WISDOM TEETH MOLARS BICUSPIDS (PREMOLARS) CUSPID INCISORS

If Joe will only keep on this routine he will escape a lot of trouble. Twice a year he should have his dentist do a professional cleaning job, to get at spots Joe might have missed. The dentist can also paint our biting surfaces with a plastic that seals out fissures against bacteria. And he can straighten and grind down teeth that don't mesh properly.

Joe has to watch the signals, too. Bleeding gums show that a break has occurred at our most vulnerable spot—the gum line. The dentist can usually spot the reason at a glance and Joe had better get to him fast. He should also remember that we need exercise. Crisp chewy foods—apples and celery, for example—stimulate our supporting structures.

It all adds up. If Joe will clean us *thoroughly*, give us *professional* cleaning twice a year, *do* something when gums bleed, we'll keep working for him for a good many years. And I know Joe would be happier with us than with a mouthful of expensive hardware.

THROAT

WHEN JOE SAYS "Good morning" at the breakfast table, the mechanical and electrical activity, and the intricate controls required to utter those words—any words—make the functioning of a space vehicle pale in comparison. When Joe swallows a spoonful of cereal, another series of precisely timed events occurs—whose precision can determine whether Joe lives or dies. I'm responsible for these miracles, yet Joe thinks of me simply as a short length of reddish garden hose connecting nose and lungs, mouth and stomach. Usually he is aware of me only when I am sore. Let's use a catchall term and call me Joe's throat.

A simple piece of garden hose? Ha! I am a vastly complex transportation system, with elaborate switching devices designed to sort and move assorted cargo: air, fluids, solids.

I was a finished piece of machinery ready to go to work at the time of Joe's birth. Had I not been, he might well have strangled on his first sip of milk. And it is my eternal vigilance that keeps him functioning normally. Let anything disrupt my timing, and he could be in deadly peril. Let Joe try to laugh while swallowing a piece of meat, for instance, and instead of routing it to the stomach I might let it slip into his windpipe—thus blocking breath. Joe would collapse from what would look like a heart attack. This so-called "café coronary" could kill him unless someone had the quick wit to dislodge the meat. In general, however, my behavior is exemplary.

Perhaps the best way to tell my complicated story is to start with my structure. Joe's neck is a real traffic jam of nerves, blood vessels, vertebrae, other bits and pieces—and my tubes. The first tube is my five-inch-long pharynx—vaguely funnel-shaped, the wide portion at the top—which begins behind Joe's nose and ends behind his Adam's apple. Next is the larynx, my main switching point, which routes traffic in correct directions and also serves as the chief component of Joe's speech apparatus. A tapered cylinder about 1 3/4 inches long, roughly bat-shaped when viewed from above, it is an intricate arrangement of nine cartilages, covered with mucous membrane and bound together by ligaments. Part of it protrudes in Joe's neck as his Adam's apple. Next down come two tubes: the esophagus leads to the stomach; the trachea, to the lungs—both about in inch in diameter.

To see how I work, let's watch Joe swallow a mouthful of food. After it is chewed, Joe's tongue maneuvers it to the back of his mouth. The uvula—that's the little red finger that hangs from the roof of the mouth at the rear—rises and helps shut off passages to the nostrils. (A spoonful of soup might otherwise dribble out of Joe's nose.) Then the tongue humps up, gives a push, and the food is on the way down.

To prevent a café coronary every time Joe swallows, I have a special mechanism. Let Joe touch his Adam's apple and swallow. He will note that it rises. This signals the closing of a flap valve (epiglottis) that sits perfectly over the windpipe. The mouthful slides safely by and into the ten-inch food tube, or esophagus. Richly muscled, the esophagus is able to produce wavelike pushes to finish the job of delivering the food to the stomach.

The food doesn't plop into Joe's stomach directly. He might have rather severe indigestion if it did. As Joe eats, I open and close a valvelike muscle where my esophagus enters his stomach, to pass along food only as fast as the stomach can comfortably handle it. If Joe wolfs his food, too much may pile up and temporarily he will have a mildly distressing sense of "fullness." Occasionally, the valve may get balky and let acid from the stomach leak upward to attack the delicate membranes of my esophagus. That can mean real discomfort. But hundreds of times a day Joe will swallow food, drink and saliva with no problems.

How do I manage speech? Joe thinks of my vocal cords as violin strings, set vibrating by air from the lungs. Actually, they are more like glistening, whitish lips that open and close as Joe's voice changes pitch, much as his lips do when he whistles. Vocal "folds" would be a more descriptive name. Controlled by an intricate muscular system, the folds open wide to produce deep sounds and narrow to slits for high-pitched sounds. They close tightly when Joe swallows—that's why he can't talk while swallowing.

Anything—a polyp, tumor, cyst or inflammation—that prevents proper closure of my vocal folds distorts speech. When Joe yells himself hoarse at a football game, his vocal folds have become tired, inflamed. The same thing happens to politicians who campaign too vigorously and to singers with too many bookings. My vocal apparatus also reflects emotions. Rage can make Joe speechless. This paralysis of vocal folds also sometimes hits grammar-school youngsters attempting a graduation address.

In a way my vocal tract—the seven inches from larynx to lips—performs much like a miniature pipe organ. As the column of air from the lungs passes through my vocal folds, the sound resulting depends on the width of the opening and also on how much the tough, fibrous vibrating bands at the edge of the folds stretch. When Joe goes from a grumble to a screech, they stretch nearly a quarter inch. (Trained opera singers' bands can stretch nearly half an inch.) What I produce is raw sound, only partially refined into speech. Lips, tongue, nasal tract and palate put on the finishing touches.

Another bit of my equipment should be mentioned here: the tonsils. I have four of these little lymph glands—and another, the adenoid, is in Joe's nasal tract. My paired faucial tonsils are

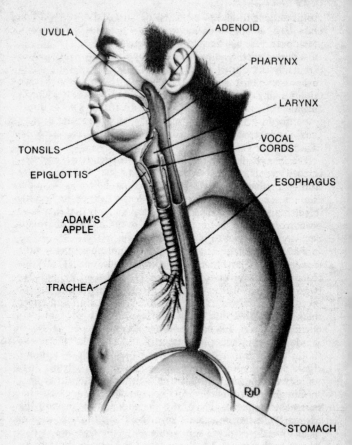

UVULA

ADENOID

PHARYNX

LARYNX

VOCAL CORDS

TONSILS

EPIGLOTTIS

ESOPHAGUS

ADAM'S APPLE

TRACHEA

STOMACH

visible at the entrance to his throat. They are the ones so often removed. The linguals, farther down, are normally the size of green peas but capable of great enlargement.

Indeed, next to circumcision, tonsillectomy is the most frequently performed piece of surgery. Doctors once thought tonsils were simply useless evolutionary leftovers and took them out thinking that it could do no harm. Today there is considerable evidence that there are more troubles of the upper respiratory tract *after* tonsil removal than before, and doctors generally agree that simple enlargement of tonsils is hardly an indication for surgery.

I've known all along that my tonsils are friends, not enemies. In their crypts they entrap invading bacteria, and phagocytes from the blood consume these bacteria much as a spider consumes a fly trapped in a web. When the tonsils become infected, inflamed and enlarged, it means simply that they have been overwhelmed. Better to nurse these valiant little guardians back to health than to throw them away.

The troubles that strike me cover an enormous range—little wonder that throat difficulties account for one fourth of all visits to doctors' offices. Via air and foods, I am constantly exposed to bacteria, fungi, viruses. My tonsils try to destroy them, and the mucous blanket that covers my tract tries to trap and sweep them away. It's unceasing warfare. When the invaders occasionally win, Joe has a sore throat.

My larynx is the chief target of these attacks. Dozens of things can irritate it—noxious auto exhausts, chimney fumes, cigarette smoke—and often it responds with laryngitis. Joe's voice becomes hoarse, drops to a whisper or fails altogether.

Coughing is one of the most important reflexes Joe has; it has been accurately described as the "watchdog of the throat." It is my major protection against an irritant—be it mucus, food or drink that "goes down the wrong way," or cigarette smoke. Whatever the cause, I try to expel the troublemaker by trapping air and letting it out with a 200-m.p.h. blast.

My larynx is also a favorite target for cancer. Fortunately, this slow-spreading cancer is one of the most easily detected and most readily cured—by cobalt treatment or surgery. Just the same, if Joe is hoarse for two weeks, he'd better get himself to a doctor.

106

If the cancer does get out of hand, then the larynx must be removed. Should this happen to Joe, he would have to learn to speak in a new manner. He would swallow air until my esophagus was filled, then release it in a controlled belch. Tongue, lips, teeth and pharynx can mold this air column into a reasonable facsimile of normal speech. Or, Joe may opt for a new electronic larynx. Not too pleasant to contemplate—nor too likely to happen, either.

In fact, for all my complexity, I perform so well that Joe rarely thinks about me. Some piece of garden hose!

STOMACH

JOE FRETS about me more than any other organ in his body. He thinks I am terribly important. Actually, I am mostly just a *convenience*—a food reservoir that permits Joe to get by on three meals a day, instead of the half dozen or more he would need without me. So far as digestion is concerned, the small intestine is the *real* champ. I am Joe's stomach. I work on protein, breaking it down into polypeptides, but even here the final job is done by the intestine, which also takes care of carbohydrates, fats and other foods.

I'm afraid I'm not a very inspiring sight. I'm glossy pink outside. Inside, I look like folds of glistening velvet. Tucked up in the abdomen at the lower rib line, I resemble a deflated balloon when I'm empty. When I'm full, I slant across the body, big at top, small at bottom, shaped roughly like a bulbous letter J. My capacity is a little under two quarts. Joe's Newfoundland dog can hold three times as much.

Although I am not as important as Joe thinks, I do perform a number of jobs that make life more pleasant for him. My lining contains some 35 million glands that may secrete about three quarts of gastric juice per day—mainly hydrochloric acid. The acid serves to activate another of my secretions—the enzyme pepsin, which starts protein digestion. Without pepsin, Joe would have a hard time with that steak he loves so much. My glands secrete other enzymes as well. One, for example, clots milk, converting it into easily digestible curds and whey.

Everyone thinks of me as a violent churn, which manhandles everything that Joe swallows. Not so. As Joe eats dinner, the food is deposited one layer at a time: the shrimp cocktail first; then the meat, potatoes and vegetables; then the apple pie. I start work on the shrimps that lie against my wall. My muscular contractions, sweeping wavelike from top to bottom, mix them thoroughly with digestive juices. Pretty soon they are a thick gruel. Gradually, I work this gruel down toward the pyloric valve, which opens into the duodenum, the foot-long first part of the small intestine.

This is a dangerous spot. If any large amount of gastric juice is dumped into the duodenum, it eats its way into the wall. That's why this is the commonest site of ulcers. Fortunately for Joe, *my* pyloric valve lets food through in little squirts—no more than can be instantly neutralized by the normally alkaline duodenum.

The mashed potatoes takes me only a few minutes to handle. Meat takes longer, and leafy vegetables still longer. How long? There is enormous variation, and much depends on Joe's mood. But four hours will probably be average for the meal described. If spinach, however, is included, it may stay around as long as 24 hours.

Fatty meals pose special problems. Suppose that at 7 A.M. Joe eats a breakfast of eggs scrambled in butter and cream, bacon and well-buttered toast. This excess of fat triggers the duodenum to produce a hormone that *slows* my muscular contractions—probably in self-protection. It can't handle such a big load of fat all at once. As a result, when Joe sits down to lunch, I may still be working on as much as a fourth of his breakfast.

Another thing that slows me is cold. If Joe eats a big dish of ice cream, I can cool down as much as 20 degrees from a normal 99°F., and everything comes to a halt for the half hour it takes

109

me to warm up again. But no harm is done. After all, I am in no particular hurry.

In fact, I lead a pretty relaxed life. While liver, heart, lungs and kidneys keep at it 24 hours a day, I can finish my work on a normal dinner by the time Joe goes to bed. So I go to sleep when he does.

A question arises: Since I digest other proteins, why don't I digest *myself*? (After all, I handle tripe quite nicely, and that is cow's stomach.) The reason is that my delicate lining is coated with a protective mucus. Scrape it away, and I turn cannibal.

I have another remarkable attribute: the way I reflect Joe's moods. When his face turns red with anger, I turn red. When he gets pale with fright, I get pale, too. When he gets excited at a football game, I react with vigorous contractions—my secretions may triple in volume. And when Joe smells a chop broiling or sees delicious-looking pastries in a bake shop, I go into action. Joe calls these hunger pains, and he just may be right.

I share Joe's depressions, too—my muscular waves all but stop, and so does secretion of gastric juice. Out of habit, however, Joe continues to eat. And what he swallows just sits there, causing distention and discomfort. In times like these, Joe would do better not to eat at all.

Stressful situations produce a different problem: They hoist acid production, sometimes to the point of causing an ulcer. Whenever Joe feels under stress, he would be wise to shift eating habits. Eating a number of small, light meals is the best way to control excess acid. Actually, Joe had a minor ulcer once, and didn't even know it. This happens to many people. Joe was in college and worried about exams. This shot my acid production up, and the acid finally found a tiny weak spot in the mucus. Joe had a few twinges of pain and attributed them to sketchy eating. But once exams were over, he calmed down, acid secretion dropped, and I got a chance to pour out mucus and heal my wound.

Aside from ulcers and cancer, very few things ever go seriously wrong with me. I can heal a scratch from a fishbone in 24 hours; on the skin, the same wound might take a week to heal. Put a piece of tainted meat in distilled water, and microbes go

STOMACH

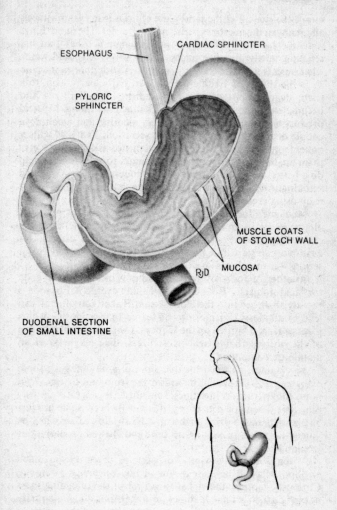

ESOPHAGUS

CARDIAC SPHINCTER

PYLORIC SPHINCTER

MUSCLE COATS OF STOMACH WALL

MUCOSA

RjD

DUODENAL SECTION OF SMALL INTESTINE

merrily to work. Put the same piece of meat in my gastric juices, and many of the microbes perish in quick order. The main things that Joe has to worry about are certain microbes that are resistant to my digestive juices. That's why Joe should watch what he eats when he travels in countries with poor sanitation.

Some things *do* irritate me: pepper, particularly; and, to a lesser degree, mustard and horseradish. I get fiery red and become engorged when these things touch my lining. My acid production is stepped up by coffee, nicotine and alcohol—a couple of martinis may double the secretion. That's why ulcer patients must lay off these things. I'm not asking Joe to give them up, but he could make life pleasanter for me—and I could do a better job for him—if he would moderate his drinking and smoking. And if he feels he needs all that coffee, he could buffer it by using cream.

Medicine? Joe loves to take it whether I need it or not. I almost never do. In fact, almost all drugs irritate me. Even in a reasonably healthy stomach like me, too much aspirin, for example, can start little pinpoint hemorrhages. But they're not serious—if the process isn't repeated too often.

Another of Joe's sovereign remedies is bicarbonate of soda for "acid stomach." But I wish he wouldn't overdo it. For soda is rapidly absorbed into the bloodstream. Taken too often, it can lead to alkalosis (far more to be feared than acidosis), which places a fearful burden on the kidneys. I wish he would take one of the nonabsorbable acid neutralizers—like magnesia or an aluminum compound.

Joe blames me for a lot that I'm not guilty of. Like those embarrassing rumbles his innards make from time to time. *That* noise comes from the intestines. I am not a gas generator the way they are. When Joe gets burpy, it is mostly because he has just had a carbonated drink or because he swallowed air when he gulped his food. If he took his time and chewed properly, this wouldn't happen.

When Joe eats unwisely, or perhaps takes on too much alcohol, I have a familiar means of housecleaning: vomiting. Curiously enough, the signal to get rid of the offending mass doesn't come from me. It comes from the brain, and sets a pretty violent chain of events under way. Abdominal and chest muscles put the squeeze on me, and the cardiac valve at the lower end of the esophagus opens wide. You know the rest.

"Heartburn," that hot spot of pain near the breastbone, is something else. If Joe has, say, drunk a little too much beer, the pyloric valve doesn't open properly and I can't empty. He burps up a gas bubble, which rises and carries along some of my irritating hydrochloric acid to the lower gullet. That's what heartburn is—nothing serious.

Joe has heard a lot about the dangers of exercise after meals, but he can forget most of this. It's true that violent exercise can adversely affect me by stopping the digestive process, but mild exercise is beneficial. A leisurely walk after a meal actually stimulates me into doing a better job.

There's one rule that everyone should follow. If any sharp pain that seems to emanate from me lasts over an hour, call a doctor! Too many people die of heart attacks thinking they are merely stomach upsets. As a matter of fact, many pains *seem* to have me as a source, particularly gallbladder pains. So play it safe—discomfort in a normal stomach usually goes away rapidly.

I've been called the most abused organ in the body—and probably I am. But I'm built for abuse. If Joe will give me a modicum of consideration, I can pretty well promise him a lifetime of trouble-free service. Let any of my neighboring organs match that offer!

INTESTINE

I AM THE UGLY duckling of Joe's anatomy. Other organs behave with quiet modesty. Not me. Constantly I remind Joe of my existence: with embarrassing rumbles, crampy pain, overactivity at one time, underactivity at another. I am Joe's 26-foot-long intestinal tract.

Joe thinks of me, vaguely, as a coiled tube looping through his body. I am far more than that. I expect I could be best described as an elaborate food-processing plant. Joe assumes he feeds *me*. Actually, I feed *him*. Most of the food he eats would be as deadly as rattlesnake venom if it got into his bloodstream. I make it acceptable, changing it into normal components of his bloodstream—food for his trillions of cells, energy for his muscles. I convert the crisp fat in Joe's breakfast bacon into fatty acids and glycerol. I turn the protein in his dinner lamb chop into amino acids. I change the carbohydrate in his mashed potatoes into sugary glucose. Without my chemical wizardry, even though he gorged himself, Joe would starve to death.

Except for cellulose—nut husks, celery strings and such—I digest virtually everything Joe eats and then pass it into his blood or lymph system. My final waste is composed half of countless millions of dead bacteria and half of the lubricating mucus I have secreted along the way, together with odds and ends I could not absorb.

My architecture is uniquely suited for the tasks of digestion. First comes my small intestine, which consists of a ten-inch duodenum, adjacent to the stomach; then eight feet of jejunum, about 1.5 inches in diameter; then 12 feet of slightly smaller

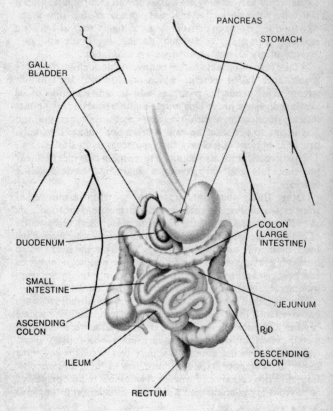

PANCREAS

STOMACH

GALL
BLADDER

COLON
(LARGE
INTESTINE)

DUODENUM

SMALL
INTESTINE

JEJUNUM

ASCENDING
COLON

ILEUM

DESCENDING
COLON

RECTUM

ileum. Next comes my big gut—five feet of large intestine. To a great degree my upper portion is free of microbes—strong stomach acids kill most of them off. But my lower portion contains a veritable microbe zoo—upward of 50 varieties with a total population in the trillions.

Digestion, of course, starts in Joe's mouth and stomach. The mouth grinds, the stomach churns; eventually, food that is about the consistency of cream soup is squirted into me through a gatekeeper valve. I may get a glass of water ten minutes after it is drunk, but a pork chop may not come along for four hours. The food the stomach delivers to me is highly acid. If I got too much at a time the acid would damage my lining and stop activity of my all-important digestive enzymes.

I take care of the acid rather neatly. My duodenum produces a substance called secretin, which empties into Joe's bloodstream. This prods his pancreas into instant secretion of its alkaline digestive juice. This juice—about a quart a day—pours into my duodenum, neutralizing acids. Let this process fail, and Joe is apt to get what he calls a "stomach" ulcer. (Actually, nearly 75 percent of ulcers of this type occur in my duodenum.) The pancreatic juice also contains three main enzymes that tear proteins, fats and carbohydrates apart into basic building blocks.

Other fluids constantly pour into me from a number of sources: two daily quarts of saliva (which moistens the food, aids in swallowing and begins the digestion of starches), three quarts of gastric juice from the stomach (which destroys bacteria in the food, clots milk and splits proteins), bile from the liver (which breaks big fat globules into minute ones the pancreatic enzymes can process) and more than two quarts of intestinal juice from innumerable glands. That's roughly two gallons of fluid!

To the naked eye, the interior of my three small-bore sections has a velvety look. A microscope, however, reveals intricate cavities and projections. In fact, if my interior were smooth it would present only about six square feet of absorptive surface. Instead, it presents about 90 square feet. Perhaps my most important components are my millions of villi—microscopic fingerlike projections on my walls. Their job is to take processed food from my contents and put it into circulation throughout

Joe's body—proteins and carbohydrates via his bloodstream, fats via his lymphatic system.

My entire length is lined with intricate sets of muscles. One group produces a swaying motion (I am only loosely attached to the abdominal wall) that churns together food and digestive juices. When I am working, there are 10 to 15 of these swaying motions a minute. Another set of muscles produces a wavelike action; the waves push my contents along a few inches, then die out. My 20-odd feet of small gut are never at complete rest.

It takes my small gut three to eight hours to process a meal. Then I pass the watery gruel that is left along to the big intestine. It extracts the water and passes it back to the blood. This is vital. If Joe lost the two gallons of fluid in a day's production of digestive juices, he would become a dried mummy in a very short time. Once water is extracted, a semisolid waste remains, which I store in the part of my colon nearest my rectum.

Normally, the water-extraction process is a leisurely one, requiring 12 to 24 hours. Many things—nervous tension, drugs, intruding bacteria—speed up passage of food. Insufficient water is extracted. Then Joe has diarrhea. Other things, including worry and bad diet, tend to bring activity to a near halt. Then Joe has constipation. Of the two, diarrhea is more serious, because it can lead to severe dehydration. Whenever Joe has diarrhea, he should drink large amounts of water.

Though I cause Joe a wide variety of miseries, most of them, fortunately, are minor. Those embarrassing rumbles that Joe hears from time to time? They're simply bubbles of gas passing through one of my loops. Mostly this is air that Joe has swallowed. But I also manufacture my own gases—mainly methane and hydrogen. Most of this gas—a little over a quart a day—I pass to the outside. When I become bloated with gas, I respond with crampy abdominal pain.

As much as any other organ in the body, I am subject to Joe's moods. Strong emotions can bring my rhythmic motions to a standstill. That's why Joe loses interest in food when angry. As far as I am concerned, it would be best for him not to eat at all until he calms down.

Like many people his age, Joe has diverticulosis, although he is unaware of it. What happens is that my walls weaken and

117

small (raisin- to grape-size) enlargements bubble out. The bubbles are no particular worry unless they become infected. Then it becomes *diverticulitis* (the *itis* ending means inflammation). Though rare, it can be serious indeed.

Enteritis is an inflammation of my lining brought on by a whole array of things: viruses, bacteria, chemicals. Symptoms are cramps, nausea, diarrhea. Joe has had enteritis many times and calls it "intestinal flu." There is no such specific disease. Generally, the inflammation subsides after a day or so of rest and a bland diet.

Ulcerative colitis—ulcers in the lining of my big gut—is another of my many ills. I don't know what causes it. If the attack is minor, with a doctor's help I can heal myself. If it's massive, the ulcer can eat through the walls of my colon to cause hemorrhage. This has never happened to Joe; if it does, he is in for serious surgery.

Spastic colon is another of my miseries. This comes mainly from stress, worry. I am very responsive to what goes on in Joe's head. Not long ago he fretted for days about losing a big contract, and I responded. My colon stiffened, went into mild spasm and failed to pass food along in proper fashion. When he calmed down I resumed normal operations.

Like most people, Joe considers himself an expert in treating his occasional bouts of constipation. Usually, I'd be better off left alone. He should remember that I am a moody organ. If I sulk for a few days, no harm is done. Joe may have an unpleasant sense of fullness, but my wastes will not poison his system.

Now that I am middle-aged—like Joe—I am no longer the efficient food handler I used to be. Once he could eat almost anything without protest from me. No longer. But even at this stage I'm only asking him to moderate his eating habits.

Frankly, we *would* get along better if Joe would only follow a few common-sense rules. He should be cautious, for example, about foods that produce gassy distress—onions, cabbage, beans and such—and should avoid heavy, fatty meals. He should eat plenty of fruits, leafy vegetables and coarse cereals, because these "bulky" foods stimulate and help me. He should

118

drink more water. Perhaps more than anything else, he should try to avoid those stressful situations that play such havoc with me.

· This is asking a lot, I know. But it is my price for operating with a minimum amount of complaint.

LIVER

JOE FRETS ABOUT his teeth, hair, lungs, heart; he is hardly aware of my existence. I am Joe's liver. When he thinks of me at all, he has no trouble visualizing me. I look like what I am supposed to look like—liver. The largest organ in his body, I weigh three pounds. Protected by ribs, I pretty well fill the upper right part of Joe's abdomen.

Despite my unexceptional appearance, I am the virtuoso among Joe's organs. In complexity I shame those headline grabbers, the heart and lungs. I do upward of 500 jobs, and if I fall down on any of the major ones, Joe had better start making funeral arrangements. I participate in virtually everything that Joe does. I provide muscle fuel for his golf game, digest his breakfast bacon and manufacture the vitamin that helps his night vision.

A big chemical company would have to build acres of plant to do my simpler jobs. The harder ones it couldn't do at all. I produce over 1000 different enzymes to handle my chemical conversions. Joe cuts his finger and might well bleed to death but for the clotting factors that I manufacture. I make antibodies that protect him from disease. The protein fragments (amino acids) made in the intestine from that steak he loves so much could be deadly as cyanide if they ever got in his bloodstream. I "humanize" them—change them from amino acid to human protein. And if there is any surplus that his body doesn't need, I change it into urea and pass it along to the kidneys for excretion.

Joe's adrenal glands produce enough salt-saving hormones to make him terribly swollen—but I destroy the excess. I even act as a kind of safety valve for the heart. On my upper side, the hepatic vein goes directly to Joe's heart. If a surge of blood comes along that might smother heart action, I swell, soaking blood up like the vascular sponge that I am. Then I feed it out gradually so the heart can handle it.

I am the great detoxifier. Shoot some poisons—such as the nicotine, caffeine and various drugs that Joe absorbs daily—into my *exit* vessels, leading to the heart, and Joe would be dead in minutes. Shoot them into my *entrance* vessels and the six to ten seconds it takes for blood to pass through me give me ample time to extract their sting.

Even the alcohol in Joe's cocktails—which but for me would accumulate in his blood in lethal quantities—I break down into harmless carbon dioxide and water. I can handle about half a highball or three fourths of a can of beer an hour; Joe could go on indefinitely at that rate without feeling any effects. But Joe tends to imbibe at a faster clip—which can leave me with an all-night job.

Some materials produced by the body are, of course, toxic if accumulated in too large amounts. My job is to keep them in check. When Joe plays golf, his muscles are burning glucose and throwing off potentially deadly lactic acid. Instead of discarding it, I convert the lactic acid into glycogen for storage. I'm a very thrifty housekeeper—no waste.

When Joe eats a chocolate bar, the cane sugar is changed into blood sugar—glucose—in the intestine. Let too much of this glucose be fed into the bloodstream and Joe will go into a coma and die—as diabetics might without insulin. I see to it that this doesn't happen. If there is too much glucose in the blood, I convert it into starchy glycogen. I can store the equivalent of half a pound of sugar this way. Then when blood sugar drops between meals—too little can be as bad as too much—I convert the glycogen back to glucose and feed it out.

It is the same with Joe's red blood cells. Each second, *ten million* of them die and must be disposed of. I salvage the breakdown products, conserving them for use over and over again in building new red cells. And some of the debris I use in making a daily quart of bile—the bitter, green-yellow digestive juice.

Normally, this fluid passes from me to the gallbladder to the little pouch called the duodenum, between the stomach and small intestine. It is released at mealtime to break down big globules of fat into small water-soluble globules that can be digested. On top of this, bile washes away fat deposits that might otherwise block my channels.

The bile that I dribble continuously into the gallbladder also contains two pigments—waste products from red-cell destruction. One is bilirubin (red bile); the other is biliverdin (green bile). Occasionally these pigments get into the bloodstream in too large quantity, and produce jaundice—a yellow staining of the skin and eyes. A symptom, not a disease, jaundice simply announces that something is wrong with me.

The trouble is one of three types. Certain diseases—malaria, some types of anemia—destroy red blood cells rapidly, and pigments from the destroyed cells accumulate faster than I can dispose of them. Obstructions in the gallbladder or ducts can also back up pigments and spill them over into the bloodstream to produce jaundice. Or perhaps my working cells may be inflamed by hepatitis or other diseases, or my channels may be blocked by fat and I am unable to excrete the pigments. Then I am in serious trouble.

Still, I have enormous reserve and regenerative capacity. Disease can destroy as many as 85 percent of my working cells and I'll continue to do my jobs. (Actually, this reserve capacity is one of my weak spots, for I can be in really grave condition before Joe gets any warning signs.) As much as 80 percent of me can be cut away, as in cancer surgery, and I'll still function normally. I can also do something that most other organs can't: I can rebuild myself, in a few months, back to normal size.

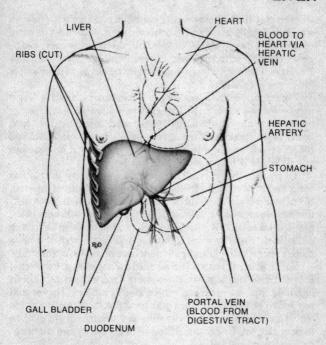

LIVER

HEART

BLOOD TO
HEART VIA
HEPATIC
VEIN

RIBS (CUT)

HEPATIC
ARTERY

STOMACH

RjD

GALL BLADDER

DUODENUM

PORTAL VEIN
(BLOOD FROM
DIGESTIVE TRACT)

Hepatitis can knock out millions of my working cells. But in a few weeks this virus infection usually subsides, and I repair the damage. In most cases, I return to normal.

Infiltration of fat may be quite serious, because the fat displaces functioning cells. If there is enough of it, I become distended, sensitive. The fat can even rupture into the bloodstream and produce vessel obstruction in vital organs. Moreover, fat infiltration is apt to precede another serious problem: replacement by nonfunctioning, fibrous tissue. I become shrunken, hard, knobby, a sickly yellowish color. This is cirrhosis—likely to be very bad news indeed.

What causes cirrhosis? A lot of things. It can follow infection or poisoning with arsenic or other drugs. But the two things that

123

seem to play the biggest role are poor diet and alcohol. The man who eats lightly, and consistently consumes 12 ounces or more of whiskey a day, is almost certain to develop a fatty liver, and to go on from there to cirrhosis. Fortunately, Joe doesn't fall into this class. There are a few wound stripes on me, but I have ample functioning cells left.

I've been called a "silent" organ, yet in times of trouble I have ways of complaining. If Joe notices undue fatigue, loss of appetite, weakness, bloating in the abdominal region, he'd better begin thinking of me. If he notices dilated, spider-shaped blood vessels on the upper part of his body, or if he becomes jaundiced, he'd better get to a doctor *fast*.

To be sure that it is me causing the trouble, the doctor has some pretty clever tests. In one, a dye (bromsulfalein) is injected. If I'm in top form, I should get rid of 95 percent of the dose in 45 minutes. In another widely used test, the pigment bilirubin in the blood is measured. If there is too much, I'm likely to be having difficulties. But the most definitive test is to push a hollow biopsy needle into me and pull out a core of my tissue for study.

So far, at least, Joe has had no need for any of this. But even if I should develop cirrhosis, the doctors have learned a lot about handling this, my most common serious problem. They would put Joe to bed and feed him a nutritious diet, high in protein. He would get liberal doses of vitamins and a warning not even to look at alcohol. Under this treatment, I'd have a good chance of getting a new start.

What can Joe do to see that none of this unpleasantness happens? He can watch his weight; when he gets fat, I get fat, too. Vitamins, particularly the B vitamins, may help. But low alcoholic intake and a sensible diet are the best bets. Given a minimum of care, I'll go along being the silent jack-of-all-trades that does so much to keep Joe in business.

PANCREAS

I AM ABOUT the size and shape of a large dog's tongue—six inches long, gray-pink in color, weight about three ounces. I reside deep in Joe's abdomen (behind his stomach and in front of his spine) in an overcrowded tenement of assorted organs that include the liver, kidneys and large intestine. Since he has eaten calves' sweetbreads, Joe knows my consistency. I am Joe's sweetbread—his pancreas.

I am a very busy organ. Without the enzymes I produce, Joe could consume mountains of food and still be malnourished. Every time he bats an eyelid, every time his heart takes a pumping stroke, cells must provide energy. I help supply the fuel to stoke the cellular fires.

Actually, I am two glands wrapped in one package, and I produce two important hormones that empty into Joe's bloodstream. My glucose, or blood sugar, is the fuel for cells, the chief provider of energy; my insulin keeps blood sugar at proper levels and sees that it is burned properly—a very critical and delicate task, I may add.

For my key role in digestion, I produce about two pints of

digestive juices a day. Not bad: 32 ounces of fluid from a three-ounce gland! When Joe's food leaves his stomach it is a highly acid gruel, or chyme. (He frets occasionally about "acid stomach," but the acid has its job to do in starting the breakdown of proteins.) This acid could spell disaster farther along Joe's digestive tract—eating away the delicate lining of the small intestine—so I must produce enough alkaline juice to neutralize it.

Let Joe sit down to the dinner table, and my tens of thousands of little saclike acini get a signal from his nervous system to start manufacturing alkaline juices. But I don't go into high gear until the chyme actually starts coming through the pylorus, the gateway from the stomach to the duodenum—that pouchy first ten inches of Joe's small intestine. As a matter of self protection, the duodenum starts manufacturing the hormone secretin, whose chemical message via the blood prods me into peak alkalinizer production.

Actually, neutralizing acid is no very impressive chemical feat. Some of my other tasks are far more formidable. If most of the foods Joe eats, for instance, ever reached his bloodstream in the form in which they are consumed, he would be a very dead duck in short order. But they don't, because I play the major role in rendering them acceptable.

For this task, I produce three talented enzymes. One of these chemical virtuosos, trypsin, initiates the breakdown of protein into amino acids, which the bloodstream can pass around the body for tissue building. Another enzyme, amylase, converts starch into sugar. A third, lipase, attacks fat globules, breaking them into fatty acids and gylcerin. Whether Joe eats a gourmet dinner or a hot dog, the results are much the same: end products almost always totally unlike the foods he forked into his mouth.

Fortunately, I have a comfortable excess productive capacity for my digestive juices. Half of my acini could do the job. Joe could even survive if my total production were destroyed. Saliva, gastric and intestinal secretions would do a job of sorts. But digestion would be a misery.

Production of insulin is my most critical task. If I fell down on this job, Joe, like millions of others, would get diabetes. (Until substitute insulin from animals came along in 1921, my

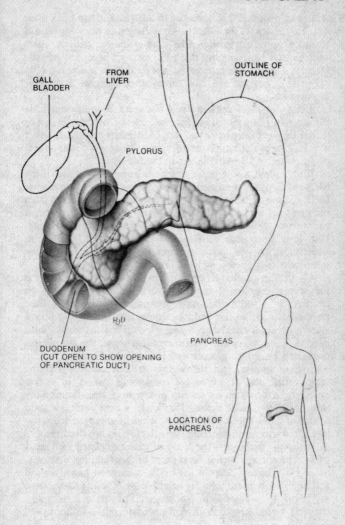

GALL
BLADDER

FROM
LIVER

OUTLINE OF
STOMACH

PYLORUS

DUODENUM
(CUT OPEN TO SHOW OPENING
OF PANCREATIC DUCT)

PANCREAS

LOCATION OF
PANCREAS

127

failure to produce this hormone in adequate quantities meant not only diabetes but death—in a lingering and unpleasant form.) To produce insulin, I have an estimated million "islet" cells scattered throughout my bulk, each an independent little factory. Despite their huge numbers, they account for only about 1.5 percent of my three-ounce weight. But their importance!

The trillions of cells in Joe's body are very efficient little furnaces, burning glucose to generate energy. My insulin sees to it that they get the precise amount of fuel they require. In other words, it helps determine the amount of glucose—about a sixth of an ounce in all—circulating in the blood.

It also plays a role in helping cells burn this glucose. If my islets suddenly went on strike, Joe's cells would try to burn other fuels. Fat would be burned. And protein would be drained from muscles to stoke the cellular fires. Joe would become cadaverous, rail-thin, wolfishly hungry and constantly thirsty. Unable to burn sugar, Joe would pass it out of his body in sweetish urine—as much as four quarts a day. These are symptoms of diabetes, which I prevent.

My insulin also has a target action on Joe's liver. The liver is the storage cupboard for any excess glucose that may be circulating in the blood. As blood passes through, the liver responds to an insulin prod by converting this excess into a starchy substance called glycogen, which is put on the shelf until needed. Then, when the system requires sugar, the glycogen is converted back into glucose and fed into the blood.

Joe, of course, can throw this delicate control of mine temporarily out of kilter by consuming sweets in excess amounts. I then step up insulin production, thus fanning the fires of cellular combustion. That's why a candy bar is a good source of quick energy. Conversely, when blood sugar drops too low, I cut insulin production—in effect, banking the fires.

Although diabetes is the No. 1 disease associated with me, I present physicians with several other brow-crinkling problems. Since I am buried deep in the body, a surgeon has a big job getting to me without injuring neighboring organs. (At one time my removal meant death. No longer. Substitute insulin and enzymes would keep Joe alive, if uncomfortable, without me.)

Whatever my difficulties, severe upper abdominal pain, often radiating to the back, is frequently present. The catch is that a number of other diseases—perforated ulcer, heart attack, gallbladder disease, intestinal obstruction—may also present much the same type of pain. Other symptoms may include diarrhea, weight loss, fatigue and jaundice.

Another common problem is acute pancreatitis. Causes of this inflammation are legion—mumps, injury during surgery on an adjacent organ, arterial disease, sustained use of alcohol. One of the commonest causes traces to my rather poor plumbing. I share with the liver and the gallbladder a common exit duct into the duodenum, and bile from the liver can back up into my duct system, injuring or destroying it. Or, a gallstone may block my exit duct, backing up my enzymes, which then start digesting *me*. Let this go on for long and it is *finis* for Joe. Indeed, acute pancreatitis represents just about as big a medical emergency as can be imagined. It kills more than 2500 persons annually.

A variety of tumors also strike at me. One of the worst is an adenoma that starts me producing excess insulin. For men in Joe's age group, cancer of the pancreas ranks as cancer killer No. 3, after lung and colon-rectum. Gallbladder disease and cystic fibrosis also often involve me.

So far, I have caused Joe no trouble whatever—except for occasional mild digestive upsets. In general, he eats and drinks sensibly, and that helps. If he keeps it up, he will very likely end his days blissfully ignorant of the commanding role I play in so much of his life.

7
Reproductive Organs

WOMB

I AM A PINKISH muscular pouch, suspended by ligaments in the lower abdomen. Roughly the shape of a small pear, I weigh about two ounces. I suppose I could be best described as a brood chamber, but that scarcely does me justice. For I can perform what may well be the supreme wonder of the universe: I nursemaid a barely visible cluster of a few cells until it becomes a complex of trillions of cells—a new human being. I am Jane's womb.

The job of providing a nursery for a new life would appear to be simple enough. Actually, it is awesomely complex—and quite frustrating for me. Each month from puberty to menopause I go through the elaborate ritual of preparing for pregnancy. This has happened—or will happen—upward of 400 times. Yet with Jane, pregnancy has occurred only three times. It is something like preparing elaborate banquets for guests who rarely arrive—400 invitations, only three acceptances!

These monthly preparations involve dazzling chemistry: construction of an intricate network of new blood vessels, new glands, new tissues. Under the prodding of the estrogen hormones from Jane's ovaries, my lining—the blood-red, velvet-smooth endometrium—thickens and my glands enlarge to provide essential nourishment for a new life. At mid-cycle, another chemical event of utmost importance occurs.

Remember, I am a hollow, muscular organ—my interior space would hold about a teaspoonful of liquid. My muscles contract regularly. But these contractions would be deadly to a fertilized egg. To relax my muscles, Jane's ovaries at mid-cycle start producing the hormone progesterone. The progesterone performs two really important functions. It helps prepare my lining for implantation, and it causes my glands (which have already been stimulated by the estrogen) to start secreting nutritional substances necessary for the nourishment of the fertilized egg in its early stages of growth.

I have three openings. Two Fallopian tubes feed into my upper portion to deliver the single egg released each month by one of Jane's ovaries. My third opening is the straw-size tunnel through my cervix, or neck. This is my entrance for male sperm, and my exit for a baby. At the time Jane's ovary is releasing its egg, my cervix steps up production of its mucous glands—to provide a stream through which the male sperm can swim toward the egg.

I am now prepared to receive the fertilized egg, and proceed with nurturing a new life. But when no fertilized ovum is delivered, all of the new tissues, glands and blood vessels I have provided must be discarded. Order is restored when Jane has her period.

My big moment came with Jane's first baby, when I finally got an opportunity to show my virtuosity. The egg had been fertilized, and cell division was already under way. The increasing cells had but one food supply during the leisurely trip down the Fallopian tube—the egg's yolk—and that was about gone by the time the egg reached me. Unless a dependable source of nourishment could be promptly found, survival prospects for this minute fleck of life looked dim indeed. Yet, as I had been so many times before, I was ready. With death just about at hand, the egg shot out tiny feelers for attachment to my endometrium. It now had a safe, warm, food-supplying home.

To feed my demanding new guest—a task that would

continue for nine months, 24 hours a day—I would be helped by one of the most miraculous and complex of all tissues, my placenta. Minute at first, it sprouted as a fleck from the fertilized ovum and eventually grew into a reddish two-pound pancake, about seven inches in diameter. No beauty, it would function as lungs, liver, kidneys and digestive tract for Jane's baby until its birth.

The baby's lifeline was its umbilical cord, which may be as short as five inches or as long as four feet. The cord contained two arteries and one vein; the arteries carried wastes from the baby to the placenta, where they diffused into Jane's bloodstream. The wastes were then disposed of by her liver, kidneys and lungs. The vein brought nourishment from Jane's blood—vitamins, oxygen, minerals, carbohydrates, amino acids. The placenta's gossamer-membrane filtration system handled these intricate exchanges even as it kept Jane's blood and her baby's completely separate. They were of incompatible types, and to have allowed them to mix would have brought on disaster.

As Jane's baby grew—at the end of the first month my tenant was 10,000 times the size of the fertilized egg—my capacity was increasing until eventually it would be 500 times its original size. My shape, too, was changing—from pear to globe to ovoid. Perhaps most important, I was growing enormously stronger. My muscle fibers increased dramatically in size and weight. But for this growth, I might well have burst with the increasing size of my tenant, particularly after it learned to flail and kick. I would need this added strength when it came time for the sustained labor of birth—exertion that would exhaust a superman.

Until about the seventh month Jane's baby changed position frequently, but then gravity took over. The head was now disproportionately heavy; so, like 96 percent of all babies, it assumed a head-down position—by far the best for birth. As my boarder increased in size and strength, I simply pushed aside anything that got in my way. I brought pressure on Jane's bladder, necessitating frequent trips to the bathroom. There were digestive upsets also, resulting from all the shoving I did on the stomach and intestines.

Reproductive Organs

By the ninth month I had taken over occupancy of a large part of the abdominal cavity. My work was about completed. I had converted an infinitesimal aquatic parasite into a seven-pound baby capable of independent life.

One fateful evening, for reasons which are not quite understood, I roused from my nine-month lethargy and began the process which would eject my tenant. I was ready to participate in the stirring drama of birth. The first, backbreaking objective was to enlarge the opening in my cervix from fingertip size up to five inches in diameter to permit passage of the baby's head. It was tedious and time-consuming, but I gradually stepped up the pace of my contractions until finally they were coming at two- to three-minute intervals, each lasting up to one minute.

All the time, I was, of course, using the baby's head as a

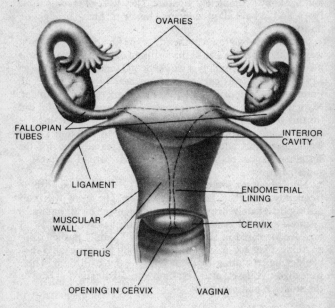

OVARIES

FALLOPIAN
TUBES

INTERIOR
CAVITY

LIGAMENT

ENDOMETRIAL
LINING

MUSCULAR
WALL

CERVIX

UTERUS

OPENING IN CERVIX

VAGINA

wedge to help enlarge the opening. My muscles were able to generate 14 pounds of thrust. Not enough. A 25-pound push was required. Jane's abdominal muscles and diaphragm gave me a helping hand. Finally, the baby emerged.

A good-sized housecleaning job remained for me. No longer needing my placenta, I expelled it. Then I had to apply pressure to exposed blood vessels to close them, thus controlling hemorrhages.

At the outset of pregnancy I weighed two ounces. My weight had increased about 16 times and I now weighed more than two pounds. In the one to two months ahead I had to exercise to get down to normal weight.

I went through this process twice more, for Jane's second and third babies. But Jane is 42, and menopause approaches. At that time my work will be finished and I will shrink back to my original little-girl size.

During most of Jane's life I will cause troubles of various kinds. I think it is safe to say that I am the No. 1 trouble spot in her body. My most familiar grief, of course, is dysmenorrhea—the crampy pain that may accompany menstruation. Fibroids, whitish growth of various sizes that sometimes develop in my muscular walls, are another of my unpleasantnesses. Like many other women, Jane thinks of these fibroids in terms of cancer. But this is largely needless fear: fibroids progress into cancer in less than one in 200 cases.

When my lining does not grow correctly or shed correctly each month, excessive or irregular bleeding results. This may have to be corrected by one of the most widely performed operations, dilation and curettage. In this surgery, instruments are used to dilate the passage through my cervix, enlarging it enough to admit a spoonlike scraper. Once excess tissue is scraped away, the trouble usually disappears.

Next to the breast, I am the commonest site for cancer to strike Jane. Fortunately, my two cancers (of my cervix and of my lining) are usually readily detectable—and, if caught early enough, over 90 percent curable. Abnormal bleeding, especially after the age of 40, is the most frequent sign of cancer of my lining. Such bleeding can be caused by other things, but if it does occur, Jane would be wise to get to a doctor immediately. And,

Reproductive Organs

wise woman that she is, Jane has a yearly Pap test for cancer of the cervix.

It is too bad that most women think of me in terms of the trouble I cause rather than the rewards I am capable of bringing. I would be grateful if they would remember that but for me and my kind they wouldn't be here. Neither, for that matter, would anyone else.

OVARY

THERE ARE TWO of us, and we hang by ligaments on either side of Jane's pelvis. We are whitish, generally almond-shaped, 1 1/4 inches long. Together we weigh barely a quarter of an ounce.

Despite our uninteresting appearance and insignificant size, my partner and I (I am Jane's right ovary) are the most feminine components of Jane's body. We play a dominant role in her life, to a great degree determining her moods, her sex drive, her general health. Indeed, it is my partner and I who transformed Jane into a woman in the first place.

Until she was about 12 years old—it might have been earlier or later—Jane was flat-chested, tomboyish and sexually immature. Then, at a signal from her pituitary gland, we supplied magic-wand hormones that set off a resculpturing of her body. Her pelvis widened; fat pads appeared on her hips; breasts began to develop; pubic and other hair sprouted; and her overall sexual apparatus began to mature.

For the next 35-odd years, we would give Jane monthly reminders of our presence, participating in the regulation of her menstrual cycle with time-clock precision. When she had her first baby, we supplied one of the two basic raw materials of human life: the egg. A few years from now, my partner and I will close up shop, and Jane's fruitful years will come to an end.

When Jane was a small child, I was a minute affair. Yet even then my colleague and I contained about half a million microscopic egg cells, or oöcytes, and each of them contained all the thousands of factors representing infant Jane's contribution to the inheritance of babies that she herself would later bear. During Jane's fruitful years, we ovaries will produce only 400-odd mature eggs capable of being fertilized—approximately one every 28 days. Why, then, 500,000 egg cells? I do not know. It's probably just another example of nature's extravagance.

How is any particular egg cell chosen to develop into a full-grown, fertilizable egg? I wish I could tell you. I cannot; I can only give a rough picture of what happens.

Early in the menstrual cycle, the pituitary gland secretes minute squirts of follicle-stimulating hormone (FSH). It is difficult to conceive of the potency of this stuff. Less than a *millionth* of an ounce a day is quite sufficient to launch a dazzling chain of events.

Under the FSH prod, several of my dormant egg cells awaken. A fluid-filled follicle forms around each of these growing cells, and the resulting bubbles, expanding rapidly, start pushing their way toward my surface.

Only one bubble will make it (unless Jane is headed for a multiple birth involving nonidentical offspring). In about two weeks, it will appear as a blister the size of a marble protruding from my surface—and representing one fourth of my volume. At this point, the pituitary secretes a spurt of a substance called luteinizing hormone, which causes the tissue-thin membrane covering the follicle to burst. The contents ooze out, and the ripe egg is swept along by a tidal wave of fluid. The egg drops gently into the funnel mouth of the Fallopian tube (see diagram) for transport to the womb, and for possible fertilization en route.

This mature egg is really extraordinary. For example, the one that produced Jane's first baby had to wait 20-odd years for a chance to play its role in the drama of creation, all the time

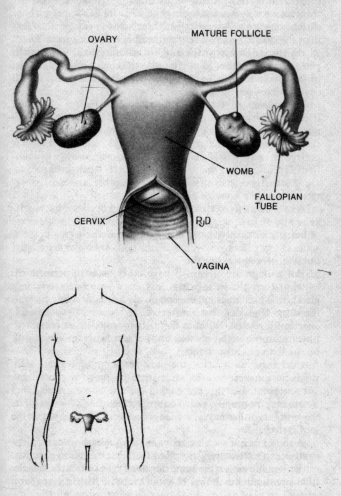

keeping alive the genetic information it contained—the 23 chromosomes that would join with 23 from Joe's sperm. The mature egg is the largest cell in Jane's body—25 times larger than the smallest human cell, the head of the male sperm. Even so, my egg is now just on the fringe of visibility: two million such glistening little globes would fit into a thimble. And it is difficult to comprehend how anything as complex as a baby could develop from anything so small.

The *quality* of the eggs I produce is a matter of prime importance. Until Jane was 15, the ability of her eggs to become mature and fertilizable was poor. Even during her peak years—roughly from 20 to 30 or thereabouts—my record wasn't perfect. In fact, 10 to 20 percent of the eggs in an average woman of childbearing years fail to develop properly when fertilized, or are rejected because of some fault or other and are either resorbed by the body or aborted.

As a woman ages, the quality of her eggs declines sharply. If Jane were to have another child right now, at age 42, her chances of bearing a defective baby would be considerably greater than when she was 30 or younger. Still, the odds are overwhelmingly in favor of a normal birth.

But enough about eggs. I have other tasks to perform of equal or even greater importance. I am a hormone-producing gland. Life itself does not depend on my hormones. But *normal* life does. Consider first the several estrogens I produce—all chemically related. Without them, Jane would have remained tiny in stature and flat-chested, and her sexual organs would still be small and nonfunctioning.

Curiously, we ovaries, the most feminine of organs, also produce testosterone—the same male hormone produced by Joe's testicles. Let this production get out of hand, and Jane would become deep-voiced and sprout a beard. We ovaries solve the problem rather nicely: we simply convert the male hormone into estrogen.

Another of our striking activities: each month we construct, in effect, an intricate *new* hormone factory. Once the egg erupts, luteinizing hormone (the same hormone that causes the follicle to burst) stimulates the crater left in me to fill with cells that are loaded with a fatty, yellowish material. This is a new gland, the corpus luteum. It manufactures a new hormone that is emptied into Jane's bloodstream. This hormone is aptly named progesterone, because it is *pro* gestation, *pro* pregnancy. Its main target is Jane's womb. Under progesterone's influence, rhythmic contractions of the womb quiet, walls thicken and a new network of blood vessels forms. A nest, and nourishment, are being readied for a fertilized egg. If no pregnancy develops, the corpus luteum shrivels and dies.

I always strive to regulate carefully my production of estrogen and progesterone. If this production is not controlled, Jane can become prey to a host of upsets, some physical, some emotional. She may retain fluid, leading to feet becoming puffy. Or, as menstruation approaches, she may become irritable, nervous, depressed, accident-prone. Fortunately, physicians have pills to correct hormone imbalance.

When Jane reaches the 45-to-50 age range, and menopause begins, we ovaries will shrink back to prepuberty size and hormone production greatly decreases. With our estrogen supply cut down, a great variety of things *can*, but not necessarily *will*, happen. A dowager's hump may form, and breasts may go flabby. For decades, our estrogen appeared to protect Jane from fatty deposits in the arteries, and from the coronary heart disease that strikes men her own age up to 40 times as frequently as women. After menopause, Jane will become almost as susceptible as men. Skin may dry, and muscles may stiffen. And she may become prone to osteoporosis, a disease that causes bones to become brittle. A slip on a rug that once meant only a bruise can now mean a broken hip.

Jane may well escape some or all of these side effects. Many women do. Should they occur, doctors can prescribe pills to replace the hormone that we have ceased to make.

The most serious threat to me is always cancer. Early cancer of the ovary is often silent, symptomless and beyond the field of the usual pelvic examination. When it *is* detected—as a tangible mass in the pelvic area—it is often too late. Although it can strike at any time, it peaks in the 45-to-60 age group. Still, I don't want to alarm Jane unduly: one million American women will

Reproductive Organs

die this year of all causes; of this total, only 1 in 100 will die of cancer of the ovary.

That about winds up my story. I have played a dominant role in Jane's life. It was my eggs that gave her the children she wanted; it was my hormones that have helped keep her in good physical and mental health. In a few years now, I will be bowing out, my task of producing another generation complete.

BREAST

I AM ONE OF THE most visible signs of womanliness.
But today many think of me as little more than a cosmetic appurtenance, a prop for the female ego. I am considerably more than that. My real reason for being is that I am capable of baffling, almost miraculous chemical conversions. I change blood into milk.

I am Jane's left breast. (As in most women, the left is slightly larger than the right.) At one time, the very survival of the human race depended on me. For Jane's primitive women ancestors, pregnancy was the normal state; baby followed baby. Breasts produced milk almost continuously during the child-bearing years and even *after* those years were over. A granny could put to her breast the infant of a woman who had died, and soon there would be milk.

In actuality, I am nothing more than a modified, and infinitely complex, sweat gland. For the first few days after Jane was born I functioned. Hormones from her mother stimulated me into producing a few droplets of "witch's milk." (So, when he was born, did Joe's breasts.) Then the hormones' effect wore off and I went to sleep. Until Jane was about 12 I was dormant. Then the magic wand of the hormones was waved. Her ovaries matured, and under the prod of their hormones I started developing. (Breasts start developing among Jane's friends as early as eight years or as late as 18 years.) Fat deposits—I am mostly fat—were laid down. I swelled. My nipple grew, and my areola, the halo around it, took on a heavier pigmentation.

My glandular structure is by far my most interesting component. I have 17 independent milk-producing units. Some women have more, some fewer. Each is shaped something like a berry bush. The berries are my tens of thousands of microscopic alveoli. The invisible droplets of milk they produce feed into the branching ducts and finally into the main stem. The 17 stems terminate in my nipple. My fat coat provides protection and insulation for these delicate structures. I also contain connective tissue to bind me together; strands of this attach to Jane's chest wall—a kind of internal bra.

I am under almost total control of hormones. Prior to menstruation, they make me swell and I become more sensitive. My really big moment came, with Jane's first pregnancy, when hormones from the placenta—which links baby and womb—awakened me. The hormone estrogen stimulated growth of my milk-duct system, and progestin prodded development and proliferation of my berrylike alveoli. Blood vessels, too, expanded their networks. Blue veins on my surface became visible. My weight doubled. As birth neared, I began a big housecleaning job. Until then, my alveoli had been filled with hard cellular material. It was necessary to dissolve this and make room for milk.

When Jane's baby was born, a new hormone came into production: prolactin, manufactured by the pituitary gland on the underside of Jane's brain. This remarkable hormone starts my milk on its way.

For the first four days after birth, I secreted a yellowish, watery fluid: colostrum. There was very little nourishment here for Jane's baby. He lost weight, and Jane fretted. But I knew what I was doing. The colostrum helped clear the baby's digestive tract of mucus and other debris. Further, in my case, it was rich in antibodies to protect the newborn from diseases that

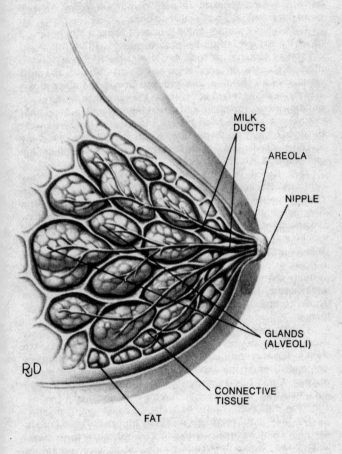

MILK
DUCTS

AREOLA

NIPPLE

GLANDS
(ALVEOLI)

CONNECTIVE
TISSUE

FAT

RJD

might be deadly—such things as measles, whooping cough, scarlet fever, which Jane had as a child. By the fifth day, Jane's baby had been cleansed internally and was ready for real nourishment. And I was ready with the perfect food.

Initially, my partner and I produced about a pint of milk a day. To achieve this, we needed many gallons of blood circulating through us each day. From the blood my alveoli plucked glucose, or blood sugar, which my enzymes, the most talented of all chemists, changed into lactose and other sugars acceptable to the infant body. It was the same with amino acids, building blocks for casein and other complex milk proteins that the baby would need for growth and tissue repair. Fats went through other transformations. From the passing blood my alveoli plucked minerals, particularly calcium for bone building, and vitamins essential to health.

Jane feared that her infant's sucking might "ruin" my contours. Her fears were groundless. Nursing would have no effect whatever on stretching the ligaments of my internal bra. She noted that my areola darkened and thickened; new lubricating fat glands had grown here to prevent painful cracking of the nipple. My nipple is composed of erectile tissue. When she put her baby to breast, this tissue hardened, providing a better grip for the hungry little mouth. The sucking brought instant response, thanks to an interesting feature of my architecture. Just under my nipple the stalks of my milk trees widen to make little cisterns—instant milk to assuage hunger pangs.

This tiny supply was soon exhausted. But my nipple is richly laced with sensory nerves. Via them, word was communicated to Jane's faraway pituitary. Within 30 seconds the pituitary responded, emptying the hormone oxytocin into her bloodstream. Once this substance reached my alveoli, gossamer muscular walls squeezed shut, forcing milk out. From now on, the baby didn't really have to suck—he could simply drink.

The milk that I produced is exactly tailored to infant needs, and that's why we breasts wish women would nurse their infants if they can. Cow's milk can be modified to approximate the needs of this stage of life. But it can never be quite the same.

Nursing has other pluses. It stimulated Jane's womb into

148

rhythmic contraction. This helped shrink it back from an envelope large enough to enclose a baby to its normal pear size. Contractions also reduced danger of hemorrhage, and gave Jane a mild sense of sexual pleasure.

At the beginning of lactation, my companion and I produced just under a pint a day—ample for a seven-pound baby. But as the baby grew, so did our production—in some women up to three quarts a day. The composition of my milk changed, too. As more calcium was needed for building bone and blood, the calcium content of my milk soared.

Finally, after about two months, Jane tired of nursing, though I could have carried on for six months without her baby needing a supplementary diet, except for some vitamins and iron. With no stimulus from a hungry little mouth, my glandular components drifted off to sleep again, and I resumed my normal weight.

What ailments am I prey to? Not many. Perhaps the commonest source of worry is breasts that are either too large or too small. Fortunately, Jane has neither of these problems. My usual weight is six ounces. Although Jane is 42 years old, I am still firm and erect. Had she not been so blessed, she could have sought the help of a surgeon. But if I were too small, virtually any reputable surgeon would have refused to inject the liquid silicone Jane hears about. However, silicone *implants* are being used to augment breasts in appropriate patients. Correcting gross enlargement is difficult, major surgery. Then, excess fat and skin are trimmed away—often many pounds of it. The breast is reshaped, and the nipple transplanted to proper position over the fourth rib.

The biggest danger I face is cancer. I am more susceptible to this disease than any other organ in Jane's body, and the most likely cause of cancer death in women. Fortunately, Jane can do a great deal to avoid this disaster. She has heard a lot about self-examination of breasts. With a little practice she can become expert at this examination, detecting lumps so small as to be missed by most doctors. She should lie down, a pillow under her left shoulder, and with the flats of three fingers on her right hand examine her left breast thoroughly. Next, she should put the pillow under her right shoulder and examine the right

149

breast with her left hand. This should be done once a month on some set date—say, two days after menstruation ceases. Further, she should watch for any depression in either breast; cancer tissue, because of its effect on other structures of the breast, can cause a slight hollowing. Any twisting of my nipple from normal position is also a signal to watch for. And any abnormal discharge from the nipple should be considered something to be checked into.

Should Jane detect a lump, she shouldn't panic. Chances that it is cancerous are less than one in three. But she should get to a doctor *instantly*—not wait, as some women do. If cancer is present and detected early, there are several possible operations that offer a survival rate of at least five years for 85 percent of patients.

Jane will soon be going through menopause. Then the things that happened to me in puberty will be reversed. I will lose some but not all of my fat deposits. My glandular structure will wither, and nearly disappear. I will shrink.

That about wraps up my story. I was put on earth for an active, productive life, and it makes me rather sad whenever I am considered primarily a decoration—however greatly admired. So I am pleased to report that there is a strong revival of interest in breast feeding on the part of many of today's young mothers. More power to them!

TESTIS

JOE HAS MIXED FEELINGS about me. For instance, he respects me as proof of his maleness. But then, he is vaguely ashamed of me. I vigorously reject this attitude. I am quite as respectable as any organ in his body, and far more remarkable than most. But for me and my kind, neither Joe nor anyone else would be here.

Nature is wiser than Joe in estimating my importance. Mostly, Joe has one gland of a kind. There are two of me. Joe thinks of me as related only to sex, but I do chemical conversions that would amaze him. It was I who changed him from a boy to a man; and, to a great degree, it is I who will decide if his old age will be tranquil or miserable.

I am Joe's left testis. Compared to other glands, I am not bad-looking at all: a glistening, pink-white oval. I weigh half an ounce and am 1½ inches long, three quarters of an inch at my greatest diameter. My function is dual: to manufacture those creators of life, the sperm cells; and to produce the hormone of maleness, testosterone. This chemical assists in construction of muscle, bone and other tissues. It helps shape Joe's mental

151

attitudes as well as his body. But for it, Joe would be soft, flabby, beardless, apathetic.

I am a very complex piece of machinery. Few parts of Joe's body do so much of importance in so small a compass. I contain a thousand tubes, each of them one or two feet long—roughly a third of a mile of them, all as fine as the finest sewing silk. These, in turn, empty into a large collecting tube, 20 feet long. It is in this duct system that I manufacture 50 million sperm cells a day. This means that every two months I produce cells that have the potential of populating the entire earth.

Of this vast number, only three have played out their roles—they created Joe's three children. Why such an extravagant excess? It is a dim reminder of life's origin in the seas. Some fish simply spray sperm into the water on the off chance that a drifting egg will become fertilized.

In addition to my duct system, I contain millions of Leydig cells. These are the producers of my testosterone. Curiously, this manhood chemical is also found in women. Joe's wife has about 1/20 his amount circulating in her blood, produced by her adrenal glands. Without it she might be frigid. With too much she would likely be masculinized.

When Joe was in his mother's womb, my partner and I were *inside* his body. Two months before birth, we descended to our present position through a little opening called the inguinal canal. Later, this can be a danger spot for hernia, if the canal doesn't completely close off after the testes have descended.

Had we failed to descend, Joe would have been sterile—and for a very interesting reason. Joe's normal body temperature is 98.6°F. At that level I cannot produce viable sperm. I must be held at a temperature three degrees lower than the rest of his body. To achieve this, I have an elaborate air-conditioning system. The sac which holds me is rich with sweat glands, which cool by evaporation of moisture. Also, as Joe has noted, in a Turkish bath I drop down. In an effort to keep me cool, the cord that suspends me has lengthened. In a cold shower it shortens, pulling me close to the body for warmth. Anything that interferes with this temperature control influences my sperm production. If Joe were to move to the tropics, it would fall; in the Arctic it would rise, since cold stimulates me. Joe once had

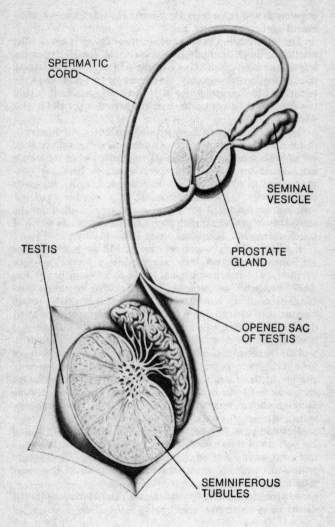

SPERMATIC CORD

SEMINAL VESICLE

PROSTATE GLAND

TESTIS

OPENED SAC OF TESTIS

SEMINIFEROUS TUBULES

pneumonia and ran a fever for a week. He didn't know it, but I ceased sperm production, and he became temporarily sterile.

The sperm cells I produce are extraordinary. They are the smallest cells in the body (in contrast, the female egg is the largest), and look something like minute tadpoles. The flailing tails are for locomotion only; the important part is the head, the creator of life. You get an idea of its size when you note that 1200 of them would be needed to cover the period at the end of this sentence.

My sperm cells have many striking attributes. All other cells in Joe's body contain 46 chromosomes; my sperm cells contain only 23. The normal allotment will be reached when the female egg contributes its 23. My sperm contains both the boy-producing Y chromosomes and the girl-producing Xs; Joe's wife produces only Xs. So the determination of whether a girl or a boy will be produced rests with me alone. In addition, the thousands of genes that each sperm cell carries decide which of his characteristics Joe passes along to his children.

Flailing furiously, sperm cells are able to swim seven inches an hour. Considering their size, this is a journey of epic proportions. A rough equivalent would be a *40-mile* run by Joe. Their prospects of piercing the relatively enormous and tough-skinned egg would be just about nil if it weren't for an enzyme with which I equip them. This enzyme dissolves away enough egg coating to permit entrance and fertilization.

Unless released regularly to the outside, millions of sperm will die of old age. If released too frequently, millions will not have had time to fully mature; they will be incapable of producing life. If frequency is excessive—say twice a day for ten days—almost total depletion takes place. My manufacturing facilities cannot keep up with such demands. It will take me weeks to get things back to normal.

It would have been helpful had Joe known this when he and his wife decided to have their first child. When months passed and there was no pregnancy, they began to worry. They thought increased frequency might be the cure. Periods of abstinence would have been better.

In a single emission, Joe will release almost fanciful numbers of the cells I have produced—up to 600 million. Even so, the

154

bulk of this huge number is still minute. Most of the fluid—about a teaspoonful—is produced by Joe's prostate and seminal vesicles. The function of this fluid is to dilute my sperm and provide nourishment and energy for movement. It contains sugar, protein, minerals.

Until Joe was 14 years old, I was relatively quiescent. In a sense, I was drowsing in the wings, waiting for my cue to go on. The cue came from the pituitary gland, up under Joe's brain. How it decided that the time had come for Joe the boy to become Joe the man, I do not know. In any case, it stirred me into a fury of activity. One of the stimulating pituitary hormones started my tubules to producing sperm; another set my Leydig cells to pouring out hormone.

This hormone—testosterone—is, in the main, a growth stimulant. Joe's parents despairingly noted that new pants seemed to hang above his ankles in a matter of weeks. In one year he shot up five inches. Baby fat became hard muscle. Joe's voice deepened. His facial fuzz was replaced by beard. Even fat glands in the skin felt the stimulus of my hormone: they became overactive, and Joe got that misery called acne.

If Joe's body was undergoing a metamorphosis, so was his personality. His emotional reactions were becoming adult. There were fewer temper tantrums; there was more confidence, greater reserve.

My hormone plays a role in sex, but not a total role. Without it, Joe would have no interest whatever. But even when it is present in normal quantities, the mind seems to play the dominant part. In adult life, the main impact of my hormone is on emotions. If I were to cease production, Joe would become irritable, fretful and sleepless. Memory would begin to fail, and he might feel the hot flashes that women often have at menopause.

I produced maximum amounts of hormone when Joe was in the 25-to-35 age group. He's 47 now, and I'm tapering off. When he is 60, I'll be at prepuberty levels. His energy and drive will lessen, but it will be time for that. I'll still produce enough testosterone for basic body needs—to keep beard growing, and such.

If Joe reaches 90, I'll still be producing sperm—but usually not in sufficient quantity to inaugurate pregnancy. Would hormone supplement assist me as Joe gets older—restore his youth? Unfortunately, things don't seem to work that way.

Can Joe do anything to assure my continued good health? Not a lot, really, except to keep generally fit. As with other organs, I welcome the stimulus of good health. I raised Joe into manhood, and I hope to contribute at least some of the chemicals essential to a comfortable and spirited old age.

8
Urinary Tract

KIDNEY

LIKE THE REST of Joe's organs, I am unappealing in appearance—reddish-brown, shaped like a bean, about the size of his fist. I am Joe's right kidney; my partner is on the other side of his lower spine. Joe has a very low opinion of me. He thinks of me simply as the producer of an unglamorous fluid—urine—and as a kind of secondary garbage-disposal unit. Brother!

Actually, I'm the master chemist of Joe's body. And Joe's intestinal tract is not his main waste-disposal system—I am. Blood passes through me continuously, and I clean and filter it, ridding it of wastes that are potentially deadly. I help prod production of red blood cells, watch over potassium, sodium chloride and other substances in his blood—a whisper too much or too little of any of them can be lethal. I control vital water balance—too much and his cells would drown, too little and he would simply dry up. I see to it that his blood is neither too acid nor too alkaline. As a matter of fact, I do so many things for Joe that the doctors still don't have a complete catalogue of my activities.

159

Urinary Tract

Look at my anatomy. Although I weigh only five ounces, I contain more than a million little filtering units—nephrons. Under a high-power microscope one of these looks something like a big-headed worm, with a twisted tail called a tubule. Untangle and stretch out my tubules and there would be 70 miles of them!

Each hour my partner and I filter *twice* the total blood in Joe's body. And it's mighty tricky filtering, I might add. I don't allow red blood cells or large particles of essential blood proteins to pass through my fine filters. Otherwise they might be lost in urine—with rapid, calamitous results. In my tubules, 99 percent of the fluid is reabsorbed. Essential vitamins, amino acids, glucose, hormones and so on are also returned to the bloodstream, but excess of any of them is discarded in urine.

Thus, if Joe has eaten two big slabs of custard pie, his urine may show enough sugar to fool a doctor into thinking he has diabetes. Let him eat a big portion of kippered herring or any other particularly salty food, and he might be in real danger if I didn't extract the salt. Salt holds water. If it were permitted to remain in the blood, excess fluid would start accumulating in the blood and intercellular spaces. Joe's face, feet and abdomen would puff up; and eventually his heart, pumping against the growing load of gallons of retained fluid, would simply falter and stop.

Potassium—mainly from meat and fruit juices—requires my equally vigilant attention. Too little and muscles begin to fail, particularly breathing muscles. A pinch too much acts as a brake on the heart and can bring it to a full halt. I simply discard the excess. Or, if Joe's diet isn't providing enough essential potassium, I hoard the existing supply like a miser.

The biggest waste I have to deal with is urea, the end product of protein digestion. Like everything else, this must be kept in precise balance. Too little means there has been damage to my upstairs neighbor, the liver. Too much and there sets in one of the ugliest diseases any doctor is apt to see—uremic poisoning. The name simply means urine in the blood. Unchecked, it can lead to shock, coma, death. As it piles up in the blood, the body makes a heroic effort to rid itself of this killer. Whitish crystals of urea "frost" may even appear on the skin as the sweat glands try to help rid the body of the stuff. Here again Joe need have no worries. He can eat all the steak he wants, for instance, and I'll handle any resulting excess of urea.

Doing my job, I produce urine continuously—about a quart a day each for my partner and me. Microscopic droplets of this waste-laden fluid pass out of each of my million tubules and feed into a tiny reservoir at my center. This connects with the bladder and the bladder with the outside. Wavelike muscular action occurs every 10 to 30 seconds, pushing the fluid along the exit tubes. At night, I slow down activity to about a third of daytime levels; otherwise, Joe would be up every hour or so.

Like everyone else, Joe has noticed that certain things step up my activity. When he is chilled, for example, the blood supply to his skin is reduced—to preserve internal heat. This means an increased flow of blood to internal organs, including me. With more blood, I make more urine.

Anger in Joe produces much the same result. His blood pressure rises, and I get an increased supply of blood for processing. Result: increased urine output.

Alcohol produces the same result via another, quite complex route. One of my main bosses is the pituitary gland on the underside of Joe's brain. It produces an *anti*diuretic hormone. Left to my own devices, I might produce too much urine and Joe would become dangerously dehydrated. The hormone prevents this. The alcohol in Joe's beer or martinis has no *direct* effect on me. But it does retard the pituitary's production of the braking hormone, so I produce urine more rapidly. If Joe has too many drinks, he becomes mildly dehydrated. That's why he craves water next morning.

Caffeine in coffee has a similar action. The nicotine in cigarettes has the opposite effect—it steps up production of the hormone. When he smokes heavily, Joe needs to urinate far less frequently.

Like Joe, I am now 47 years old and beginning to show my age. I am a candidate for a lot of ills—floating kidneys, for example. Joe needn't worry here, mainly because he does watch his weight. Normally, kidneys rest in a bed of fat. When the very obese reduce, much of this bed disappears, anchoring tissues stretch and the kidneys begin to drift.

Urinary Tract

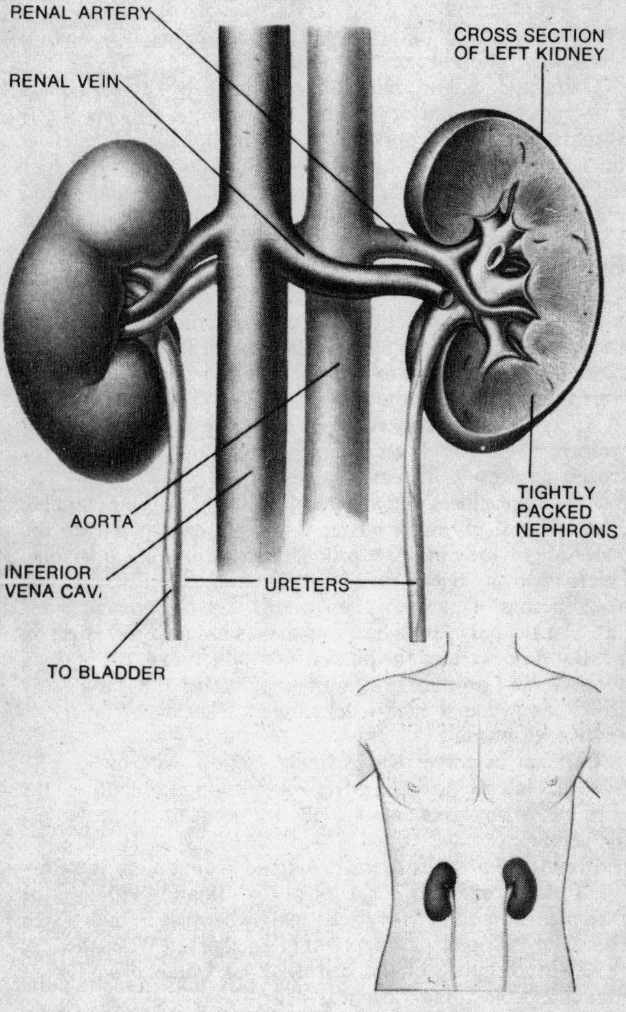

RENAL ARTERY

RENAL VEIN

CROSS SECTION OF LEFT KIDNEY

TIGHTLY PACKED NEPHRONS

AORTA

INFERIOR VENA CAVA

URETERS

TO BLADDER

Joe has also heard of kidney stones. These may occur when urine is too concentrated—calcium salts, uric acid and the like simply crystallize out. The stones may be tiny "gravel" size and pass to the outside without Joe's even being aware of them. If they grow larger—say to the size of a pea—the story may be quite different. As they try to pass through my exquisitely sensitive ureter, the tube leading to the bladder, they can produce intense pain. In extreme cases, stones may grow as large as a grapefruit. These big ones require surgery.

Joe may avoid the formation of kidney stones by maintaining an adequate fluid intake. The equivalent of nine glasses of water a day—most of which comes from food—is about right. Meat is 50 percent water; bananas are 90 percent, watermelon, 93 percent.

My really big problem is damage to my filters, or nephrons. Infection is one villain. It usually creeps up from the urinary tract below. Fortunately, such infections are usually promptly controlled by antibiotics. Large burns can cause my nephrons severe damage—wastes from destroyed tissue pile up more rapidly than I can dispose of them, and blood essentials weep from wounds faster than I can replace them. Injury—from a kidney punch or an auto accident, for example—is also troublesome to my nephrons, as are many drugs and poisons.

As a rule, all these things cause only temporary damage—readily repairable, since I have striking regenerative powers. A steady concern, however, is the hardening of the arteries that seems to be a part of the aging process. My arteries harden, narrow and become inelastic—just as they do elsewhere in the body—thereby reducing my blood supply. In time, Joe's heart may lose some of its pumping power. This, too, cuts my blood supply. In these situations I begin to fall down on my job of laundering blood. I let toxic wastes pile up, and allow sodium, potassium, chloride and other things to get out of normal balance.

Some of this already has happened to Joe; quite a few of my nephrons have been destroyed. Fortunately, my partner and I have a big reserve capacity. We can do a pretty good job even if 90 percent of our nephrons stop functioning. Wise medical and dietary management can still provide years of life if such a point is reached. This means keeping an ever-vigilant eye on salt, potassium and other substances in food to maintain them in exact balance. And fluid intake must be exactly balanced with losses via lungs, perspiration and urine. There are drugs, too, that now help in situations once considered hopeless.

The medical profession has come up with some remarkable tests to determine the exact nature of the problem when I give trouble. The basic test, of course, is the urinalysis. Does the urine contain protein? It shouldn't, except in the most minute amounts. The presence of protein indicates that my filters are letting it escape from the blood.

Are there "casts"? When my tubules are inflamed, solid matter (cells, fats, proteins) solidifies to the exact shape of the tubule, and from time to time these casts are flushed out by urine.

Blood, too, helps in diagnosis. Does it contain excess urea? If so, I'm falling down on my job of ridding Joe of protein wastes. In another test, a dye is injected into Joe's bloodstream. The time it takes me to pass this material out in urine is measured: the longer it takes, the more trouble I am in. There are dozens of tests like these.

What can Joe do to ease my jobs? Watching weight and blood pressure are two things. Exercise helps, but not violent exercise. Overworked muscles produce excess lactic acid, which is a burden on me. An extra glass or so of water a day helps; most people drink too little fluid. If Joe's urine becomes cloudy, smoky or mahogany-colored, he should get to a doctor fast. If he notes puffiness of face, nausea, blurred vision and weariness, it's likely that I am ailing—and want immediate attention.

I'm not asking Joe to dwell on me, or to fret about me. I'm asking only that if he hears a cry for help from me he listen attentively. I'm far too important to Joe for any trifling.

BLADDER

HANDS DOWN, I would win any contest for the least glamorous organ in the human body. I am a constant source of annoyance and embarrassment to Joe. I am a sleep spoiler—getting him out of bed on cold nights. At important business conferences I speak with greater authority than Joe's boss or his clients. They may have important messages, but mine take precedence. I don't ask for attention. I demand it. I am Joe's bladder.

Joe thinks of his intestine as his main waste-disposal system, but he's wrong. That tract might go on strike for a week—or in extreme cases for several weeks—and Joe wouldn't necessarily face any grave danger. But let his urinary system close shop for more than a few days and he would be in real trouble.

When full I am roughly the shape of a punching bag. Bladder capacity varies with individuals—from 6 to 24 ounces. Joe is in the normal range—about a pint. Day and night, kidneys dribble urine into me as they filter wastes from blood. It comes via two tiny ureters—tubes about the size of pencil leads and 12 inches long.

Urinary Tract

My exit to the outside is the pencil-size urethra. The amount of fluid I empty through it each day varies tremendously—from one pint to two gallons. Joe is about average—three pints. But this can vary. The volume is largely determined by fluid losses from sweat glands and lungs. When Joe perspires my production falls. Fortunately for Joe, urine production also drops during sleep to about a quarter of daytime levels. Otherwise he wouldn't get much rest.

When I empty, muscles at the top contract first, then those below add their squeeze. In effect, I wring myself out. How often I do so is determined by many things. Worry, anxiety and fear hoist blood pressure and thereby step up kidney activity and production of urine. Mental stresses, the excitement of a ball game or anger tend to tighten my muscular walls. I may not be full but wish to be relieved just the same.

When Joe's wife, Jane, was pregnant, her baby in effect sat on her bladder, and under this constant pressure her calls were many. Joe notes that on cold days I give frequent distress signals. What happens is this: To conserve heat, his bloodstream detours skin blood vessels. More goes to internal organs. As kidneys filter more blood they produce more urine. Certain condiments also irritate me—mustard, pepper and ginger particularly, and even tea and coffee. Alcohol is similarly irritating, particularly the flavorings in gin.

An examination of my urine can reveal an enormous amount about what is happening elsewhere in Joe's body. Everything considered, it is probably the most valuable of all medical tests. If Joe notes that his urine is persistently cloudy, malodorous or discolored, he would be well advised to consult a physician. Is urine water deep amber? This may mean that the kidneys are doing *too* good a job of concentration, or only that Joe has been playing tennis and sweating so heavily that he hasn't a lot of fluid left for the kidneys to dispose of. Is it cloudy? This may indicate kidney sickness or can be meaningless. Urine tends to cloud after heavy exercise. Is there blood in urine? This can be deadly serious. If he ever finds this, Joe should get to a doctor fast.

Today's doctors lean heavily on elaborate urine testing. If the specific gravity of the fluid—its weight in relation to a similar amount of pure water—is too low, the kidneys are doing a poor

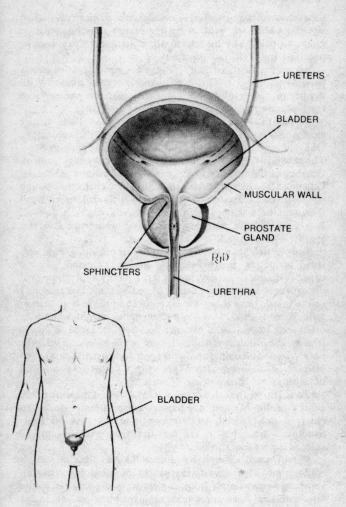

job of concentrating wastes; if too high, it may mean the patient is dehydrated. Uric acid? A high level may indicate stones or gouty kidneys. Also associated are heart and kidney disease, psoriasis and endocrine disorders.

To some extent, virtually all organs empty waste or excess production in urine. This is particularly true of glands. With pregnancy, for example, surplus female hormone passes out of the body in urine. Hence urine tests for pregnancy.

Urination is considerably more complex than simply emptying a bag of water. I have two valves called sphincters. One is at my base and opens automatically when I am distended. The second is a little lower and is under voluntary control. Opening of the first makes Joe conscious of a desire to urinate. Opening of the second sets events in motion. Controlled opening of this second valve must be learned in early childhood. Until then a mother has a bed-wetter on her hands. At death, Joe will lose control of this restraining valve and become a bed-wetter again.

Bed-wetting has a variety of causes. For one thing, I am very small in infants. But between the ages of two and four my capacity doubles. Anxiety, insecurity, a variety of psychological disturbances are common causes of bed-wetting. For reasons I can't explain, these things are far more common in boys than in girls. When a child moves to a strange, new neighborhood, he often feels insecure and resumes bed-wetting. Once he makes friends, the problem vanishes. Incontinence is general with the paralyzed and is common with the aged. Neurogenic (paralyzed) bladder is another matter. This usually traces to congenital brain or spinal-cord damage of some type.

To a degree, the force of my stream is a good measure of my general health. My exit tube passes *through* Joe's prostate. An enlarged or diseased prostate can reduce or cut off flow. Strictures—traceable to venereal or other diseases—do the same. Tumors can also be involved.

It may seem strange, but Joe could get along quite well without me. If a devastating cancer required my removal, surgeons would simply hook ureters from the kidneys to the large intestine. Then Joe would mimic the birds—which do not have urinary bladders.

168

While I reflect troubles elsewhere in Joe's body, I have my own particular set of ailments. Stones often form in me. They can block both my entrance and exit tubes. That means exquisite pain. Urine backing up in kidneys long enough can lead to uremic poisoning and death.

Bladder stones are composed of minerals precipitated out of urine that for one reason or another has become too concentrated. For some very complex reasons, stones are far commoner in warm climates than in cooler areas. Lack of exercise also seems to lead to them. They vary in size. Some may be tiny bits of "gravel" that pass readily to the outside. But, in extreme cases, stones have grown to 14 pounds!

Curiously, stones as large as oranges may well be tolerated for years, giving rise to no serious symptoms whatever. So long as they don't have jagged edges to injure my tissues, and so long as they don't block my vital passages, I can live with them. When stones do cause difficulties, surgeons may operate to remove them. Or, they may pass a specially equipped cystoscope through my urethra. This small tube is equipped with lenses for observation and has nutcracker jaws to crush stones to passable size.

All in all, cystitis is my biggest problem. Microbes creep in to cause a very uncomfortable infection. At one time or another virtually all women experience this. The reason they are so much more prone to it than men is obvious. The female urethra is only an inch or two long. The male tube, passing through the penis, is far longer, 8 to 12 inches. Thus, in women, microbes from the outside have only a very short distance to travel to reach me. Fortunately, cystitis is more of a nuisance than a deadly serious disease—leading to frequent urination, burning, and a general feeling of discomfort—and can usually be corrected with antibiotics or sulfa drugs.

From all the attention I demand, and all the trouble I cause, I might be expected to rank high in importance among Joe's organs. But I must confess that I really don't amount to much. In final analysis, I am simply a cistern, regularly filled, regularly drained. Just the same, I will continue to boss Joe for the rest of his days.

PROSTATE

I AM ONE OF THE hot spots in Joe's body, a design
nightmare for which Nature should hang her head.
Red-brown, about the size of an English walnut, I produce a
variety of grief. I can disturb Joe's sleep by requiring several
trips to the bathroom each night—or kill him with uremic
poisoning. If Joe lives long enough, I will become a cancer site
far surpassing the lungs in importance.

Fortunately, I have some good points. I make an important contribution to a normal sex life for Joe. To a great
degree, the very existence of the human race depends on me. I
am Joe's prostate gland, the principal storage depot for his
seminal fluid; without me, chances of a pregnancy would be
about zero. At each ejaculation, Joe's testicles provide
something over 200 million sperm cells. My task is to produce a
fluid that will dilute them thousands for one. And a very special
fluid it is, containing proteins, enzymes, fats and sugars to
nourish the fragile sperm, alkalinity to overcome the deadly
acidity of the female tract, and a watery medium in which the
sperm can swim toward the female egg.

I nestle in Joe's lower abdomen, right at the neck of the

bladder. Until Joe reached puberty, I was about the size of an almond. Then, along with the rest of his body, I got the hormonal signal to change Joe from boy to man. I grew to my present size, and my little grapelike clusters of secretory glands began manufacturing seminal fluid for storage in my well-muscled pouch.

In periods of sexual excitement, how do I know when to empty my contents? I don't. I simply follow orders that come from the lower end of Joe's spinal cord. Many complex things happen in my area when the signal arrives. The sphincter valve at the bladder neck squeezes tightly shut so there will be no escape of urine. Waves of muscular contractions sweep over me. The same is happening to the two seminal vesicles, the storage depots for sperm, which lie adjacent to me and look something like two linked peanuts. The vesicles contribute about 20 percent of the seminal fluid, and I the rest, for a total of about a teaspoonful. The mixture is projected out through Joe's urethra, or urine tube, to fulfill whatever destiny awaits.

As I said before, I am an architectural nightmare. I have three lobes, or sections, enclosed side by side in a capsule. The small urinary tube that empties Joe's bladder passes over the middle lobe; anything that happens there to swell the prostate—infection, inflammation, cancer—can enlarge these lobes and thus obstruct the flow of urine, causing a wide spectrum of misery. With partial obstruction, urine backs up in the bladder and becomes a stagnant pool; bacteria often invade the pool, multiply and cause serious infection. Worse still is complete blockage. Then urine may back up all the way to the kidneys and spill over into the bloodstream, causing uremic poisoning—an ailment capable of bringing a slow death.

As Joe grows older and production of testicular hormone diminishes, it would be logical to expect me to shrink back to boy size. Strangely, however, the exact opposite happens. I grow larger and, in extreme cases, may become as big as a grapefruit. This enlargement can be either cancerous or "benign"—although there is seldom anything very benign about it.

So far, Joe has been fortunate; I am still normal-sized. But soon, almost inevitably, the slow swelling will start. When Joe reaches the age of 50, he will have a 20 percent chance of an enlarged prostate; at 70, it will be 50 percent; and at 80, it goes to

80 percent. What causes the enlargement? I haven't the slightest idea. But it seems to have something to do with sex hormones since it rarely occurs among eunuchs.

By itself, the enlargement of Joe's prostate doesn't necessarily mean serious trouble. But should I enlarge enough to put the squeeze on his urethra, his urine stream will decrease in size and force; if infection starts up there will also be a burning sensation. Other symptoms: frequency of urination and the unpleasant—and accurate—feeling that his reservoir hasn't been completely emptied.

When these things happen, I urge him to see a doctor *immediately*. The chances that he will need surgery for my removal are small—about one in 20. The doctor will want to determine whether there is infection present, or inflammation. Almost certainly, he will advise the avoidance of alcohol, pepper, coffee and tea. All these things pass irritating substances along to the urine—and this irritation can close the already constricted urethra.

If closure takes place, a real emergency is at hand. The first problem is to get the urine tube open and establish drainage. This is done by passing a rubber tube through the urethra to the bladder. From here on, the surgeon has several options. He can remove me surgically, if I am too large. Or he may decide that a simpler procedure will solve the problem. In this case he slips an instrument, about the size of a pencil, into the body via the urethra. This lighted tube has a viewing device and a tiny, electrically actuated cutting loop with which to scoop out obstructing tissue. One further option is to freeze blocking tissue with liquid nitrogen. Later, the frozen tissue dies, sloughs off and passes out with the urine. Joe fears these procedures, thinking they spell the end of his manhood. Not so. Four out of five men remain sexually capable after prostate surgery for a benign enlargement, though most often they are sterile.

Benign enlargement, however, is not my most dangerous problem. Cancer is. My cancers are apt to be particularly nasty, giving no early warning signals. By the time 19 out of 20 men with prostate cancer get to the doctor, it is too late for the cure surgery offers. Nor is the disease a rare one. By the time Joe is 50 he will have a five percent chance of having prostatic cancer. By 70, his chances will be 50-50.

172

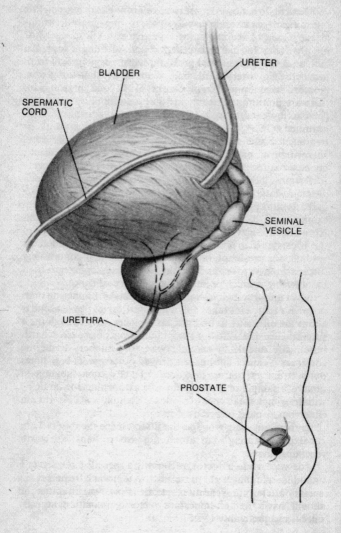

BLADDER

URETER

SPERMATIC
CORD

SEMINAL
VESICLE

URETHRA

PROSTATE

These figures, however, are not as alarming as they seem. For one thing, my cancers are usually slow-growing—only occasionally are they of the exploding type that can kill in weeks or months. Thus Joe has an excellent chance of going to his grave with an active but nonfatal prostatic cancer, dead instead from heart disease, artery hardening, diabetes or something else. Another point: even when my cancers are beyond surgical help, there are nonsurgical treatments that are often lifesaving. For growth, my cancers seem to require the stimulus of male sex hormone. Once this stimulus is removed—by castration or treatment with female sex hormone—pain often disappears, energy returns, normal tasks can be resumed. Radiation shrinks my cancers, too, and combines well with hormone treatment.

Despite all this medical skill, however, 17,000 American men die of prostatic cancer each year. What can Joe do to avoid being in this group? Fortunately, a great deal. When he has a physical examination, he can ask for a serum acid phosphatase test. Normally, the enzyme detected by this test is largely confined to the prostate; if it is found in the blood in any considerable amount, the presumption is that the capsule that contains my three lobes has broken and that my enzyme is escaping into Joe's bloodstream—which points to the presence of cancer.

Most important, Joe should have a rectal examination once or twice a year. This takes only a minute during a physical and is about the *only* way to find prostatic cancer early enough for a surgical cure. If the doctor's examining finger discovers a hard, button-size nodule in my otherwise soft, rubbery tissue, he considers it cancer until he has proved otherwise. (Three times out of five, these buttons *are* cancer.) To be certain, the surgeon obtains a sample of the button tissue by opening Joe up or by withdrawing a small core of tissue with a hollow needle. If I am cancerous, I must be removed in toto.

Is there anything else Joe can do to escape the misery I am capable of causing? I'm afraid not. So perhaps it's worth repeating myself:

Joe *must* go to a doctor, preferably a specialist, whenever I announce trouble with my classic symptoms: frequency of urination, a burning sensation, retarded flow. And, of course, he should have that all-important rectal examination at least once—and preferably twice—a year.

9

Structural and Other Body Components

SPINE

I CAN CAUSE JOE more double-barreled misery than any other part of his body. I am Joe's backbone, and he has some pretty wild ideas about me. He thinks of me as a series of "joints" that go "out"—out *where*? I ask. Every year or so, when I flare up, Joe has me pummeled, heated and drugged—none of which does much good. The pains I give him are simply my response to the bad treatment he gives me. Ironically, there is very little wrong with me that Joe couldn't fix himself. He need never have another backache.

Trouble in my department began when Joe's ancestors decided to stand erect. Instead of a nicely balanced suspension bridge, I became a tent pole. And quite a versatile tent pole at that: one that can bend, twist, swivel a head and support most of the body's weight.

I also must provide security for Joe's 18-inch spinal cord. Let anything serious happen to this whitish, half-inch-thick cable and Joe will likely spend the rest of his life in a wheelchair, for the millions of messages which fly back and forth along it direct all his activities below the neck level. I protect the cord with

177

three layers of sheathing, a fluid bath to take up shock, plus a bony housing. Thirty-one pairs of nerves branch out from the cord. Almost half are sensory, which convey information to the brain; the rest are motor, which transmit orders from the brain to the muscles. In some situations, the cord even does its own thinking. Joe's finger touches a hot stove. There's no time to waste conveying this information to the brain. My cord orders a reflex action—and the finger is jerked away.

The chances of my cord ever causing Joe any trouble are rather remote. But my 33 vertebrae and their supporting structures are another story. A wide range of things can cause pain here: trouble with kidneys, prostate or liver; arthritis and various infections; even emotions. For example, several times Joe has had big worries that nagged at him for days. He developed a dull backache. He didn't connect my hurting with his worries. As usual, he thought I was "out." What was really happening was this: strong emotions tighten muscles; mildly tensed for several days, my muscles simply grew tired and announced it with dull pain. Once Joe stopped worrying, I ceased hurting.

If Joe would study my structure—really an engineering marvel—he'd get a better idea of what causes backache. Starting at the top, I have seven cervical vertebrae, which are capable of an extraordinary range of movement. In addition to supporting Joe's head, they can twist to let Joe look down at the ground or up at the stars. Laterally, they permit 180 degrees of motion, letting Joe look over either shoulder.

The 12 thoracic or chest vertebrae, which come next, aren't capable of such a wide range of movement; there's no need for it. The ribs are hooked to these. Trouble in this area is rare.

At the lower end are five heavy lumbar vertebrae, which carry most of Joe's weight; five sacral segments, which are fused together to form the coccyx—all that is left of the tail once sported by Joe's forebears. This lower area, particularly around the fourth and fifth lumbar vertebrae, is the big trouble spot.

When Joe was born, I was more or less straight. Then, when he began to hold his head erect, my vertebrae took on a curve in the neck area. Another curve developed lower down when he began to toddle. Result: I have a vague S shape today. Actually,

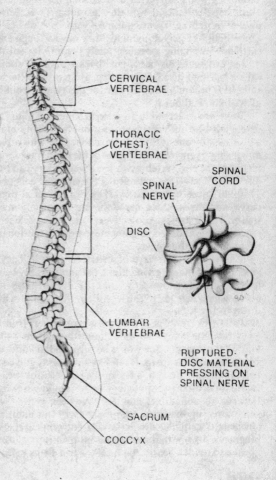

CERVICAL
VERTEBRAE

THORACIC
(CHEST)
VERTEBRAE

SPINAL
CORD

SPINAL
NERVE

DISC

RUPTURED·
DISC MATERIAL
PRESSING ON
SPINAL NERVE

LUMBAR
VERTEBRAE

SACRUM

COCCYX

this is far better than a perfectly straight spine, for the arches act as shock absorbers.

There are other shock absorbers as well—there have to be. If vertebra ground on vertebra, absorbing 100-pound jolts with every step Joe takes, I wouldn't last long. Thus, between each pair of vertebrae, I am equipped with cushions called discs. Something like jelly doughnuts, they have a tough envelope of cartilage containing a resilient, jellylike interior substance.

Joe attributes his occasional back trouble to something he calls a "slipped disc." He's wrong. He has never had one. But since he *is* becoming a candidate for this type of trouble, he may as well know about it.

Discs are susceptible to several kinds of injury. A really severe jolt—an auto accident, a serious fall—can simply squash a disc, usually one at the bottom of the spine. This often calls for major surgery, involving removal of the remnants of the disc and fusion of the two vertebrae. A less severe injury can rupture the disc's tough envelope, permitting the enclosed jelly to ooze out. This can cause acute misery. The disc material presses on a nerve, and the irritated nerve throws one of my muscles into spasm. This spasm is a protective effort. The muscle senses that I am in trouble and tries to splint me to prevent motion that might cause additional damage.

Muscles in spasm have other effects as well. They twist the victim out of shape, giving him a list and possibly bending him forward. Almost always a ruptured disc irritates the sciatic nerve, which extends to the legs. Pain then radiates all the way down to the toes.

Joe's back troubles, as with most people, stem from weakness and stretching in my elaborate supporting system—400 muscles and 1000 ligaments. Joe would be surprised to know what poor shape my muscles are in. He thinks his Sunday golf keeps him in trim. It doesn't. Look at a few of the burdens Joe thrusts on me:

He is beginning to spout a paunch—about ten extra pounds. Because his abdominal muscles have been getting weaker for some time, my back muscles must carry this additional load. (Incidentally, that's why Joe's wife got a backache with each pregnancy—from that extra load up front.)

Even after 47 years, Joe hasn't learned to sit properly. He

sags into overstuffed sofas and chairs. He may be resting, but my muscles aren't. They're working overtime trying to keep some order within my vertebrae. And, as far as I am concerned, Joe's desk chair is a horror—a swivel affair with soft cushions. Day in and day out it puts the same strains on the same sets of muscles. I'd be better off if he used a straight kitchen chair and rested me whenever possible by crossing his legs.

Joe thinks of me as a lever. I'm not! Arms and legs are levers. Ideally, I should remain straight. If he wants to throw a log on the fire, or pick up something heavy, he should squat, letting his legs do most of the work.

As a matter of fact, Joe would do well to avoid any heavy lifting; my weakened muscles are already working at capacity; and overloading, even heaving on a stuck window, can cause serious strain or disc trouble. Joe should realize that the cushions between my vertebrae aren't as tough as they used to be. Actually, they started downhill when he was about 20, getting softer, losing resilience. Even so, they are quite capable of giving years of perfectly adequate service. But they are no longer capable of taking abuse.

Mostly, I've talked about pain in my lumbar region. I can cause trouble up above as well. On rare occasions, discs in the neck can rupture, radiating pain down the arms. The stiff neck that Joe sometimes gets is traceable to stretched or inflamed muscles or ligaments. The worst trouble of all, of course, is the broken neck. I can give Joe some advice here. If he ever happens to be first at the scene of an auto accident, he should never touch a victim until he is sure that person can move arms and legs. To lift the head of someone with a broken spine may do additional damage to the cord and cause permanent paralysis.

With age, bones grow weaker. This is beginning to happen to my vertebrae; calcium is draining away. As my discs soften, and vertebrae become less dense, Joe's back will arch more. He'll get the slight humpback of old age.

Joe can avoid a lot of misery in the years to come if he only gives me the care I require. For one thing, he can check his posture right now. Let him stand as firmly as he can against a wall, then slip his hand behind the small of his back. There should be very little room. The greater the space there, the more

Structural and Other Body Components

I am curving—probably because of muscle weakness—and the more likely I am to cause Joe trouble.

Muscle weakness—that's really the key to the whole thing. Joe should see his doctor to learn something about strengthening exercises. A few minutes a day spent exercising, plus more attention to posture and thoughtful choosing of beds (firm) and chairs (firm), are a small price to pay for my well-being. If Joe treats me right, I'll treat him right.

THIGHBONE

JOE THINKS OF US bones as dead material, simply an inert Tinkertoy framework for his living body. To a degree he is right. Without us he would collapse into a blob of jelly, unable to walk, talk or eat. But we are anything but dead or inert. We are *organs*, with a host of responsibilities beyond supporting Joe's body. We contain virtually *all* of the body's mineral supply—99 percent of his calcium and 88 percent of his phosphorus, for example, plus smaller amounts of copper, cobalt and other essential trace elements. As a high-turnover warehouse we operate 24 hours a day, moving inventory in and out.

We also have a busy manufacturing division—our marrow. In a single minute, 180 *million* of Joe's red blood cells die of old age. Joe's spleen and his liver supply a few replacements, but the vast bulk come from us. In the spongy interiors of our marrow chambers we also produce most of the white blood cells that protect Joe from infection.

I am Joe's right femur, or thighbone. I will speak for the other bones because I am the largest, longest and strongest—strong

183

enough, in fact, to bear the weight of a compact car. We bones are a big family. There are 206 of us in Joe's body—some people have more, some less. As a matter of fact, Joe had more bones as a child than he does today. When born, he had 33 vertebrae in his spine. Then four of the lower ones fused to make the coccyx and five fused to form the sacrum. He might have had 11 pairs of ribs, or 13. Actually, like most people, he has 12.

We bones come in all sizes and shapes: from the tiny stapes bone in Joe's middle ear (which makes hearing possible) all the way up to me. My job, shared with my partner in Joe's left leg, is to carry his body weight. We bones are bound together by ligaments. Tendons hook us to muscles; like strings on marionettes, they make motion possible.

We are made of two basic types of tissue: *cancellous*, which is light and porous, and *compact*, which is dense and superbly strong. Joe's spine and pelvis consist mainly of the first type, while I am primarily of the latter, as are other leg and arm bones. We discovered, millions of years before today's construction geniuses caught up with us, that weight for weight, a tube is stronger than a rod. This principle makes me, ounce for ounce, stronger than a solid piece of steel.

When Joe was born his bones were softer. This, of course, facilitated birth. The intricate process of calcification made them harder. We bones contain millions of cells called osteoblasts, which extrude a fibrous protein—firm but pliable—called collagen. Among the fibers are minute air spaces containing a gluelike mixture called ground substance. As these spaces fill in with microscopic particles of mineral (mainly calcium, phosphorus and carbonate), bone is formed. This job completed, Joe's legs became strong enough to support him.

During Joe's boyhood, we bones had to support his body *and* grow ourselves—quite a task, something like enlarging a house without disturbing the occupants. During this period, certain areas at the ends of the long bones were composed of soft cartilage. New cartilage continued to form while the older, inner levels hardened into bone. But as Joe matured, those areas of cartilage solidified and no further growth was possible.

While we can't grow in length, like muscles we can enlarge or lose mass, grow stronger or weaker. Let Joe take up weight lifting and I would become stronger, denser, thicker; let him lie in bed for several months and I would weaken.

My role in storing and releasing calcium is crucial. It is via the blood that I transact all of my business—I have, of course, my own surprisingly rich supply of blood vessels. I expose my mineral crystals to the current, plucking excess calcium from the blood or supplying it when there is a lack. The surface of crystal we bones expose to the bloodstream is vast; all flattened out, it would cover 100 acres of land!

Our hoard of calcium is relatively enormous—2.2 pounds of it. But at any given moment there is only 1/40 ounce of calcium circulating in Joe's bloodstream. Yet this tiny amount plays a key role. Without it, no impulses would travel along nerves, and blood would refuse to clot. Muscle contraction would cease—and so would Joe's heartbeat. Too much calcium can be just as serious, possibly contributing to the formation of kidney stones. Next steps: uremic poisoning and death.

I mention these grisly facts simply to indicate how important it is that I have a supply of calcium ever ready, and that I feed *exact* amounts of it into Joe's blood. The principal controls are glands in Joe's neck. If blood levels of calcium drop, the parathyroids start secreting a hormone—my go signal. Too much calcium, and a hormone from his thyroid causes me to absorb calcium.

Joe thinks the only problem we bones face is fractures. As a matter of fact, being broken is generally a minor worry. Breaks come in four basic forms: closed, where the break is clean and the bone does not protrude through the skin; open, where it does protrude; green-stick, where the bone splits longitudinally without breaking entirely; and comminuted, where bone is shattered into small fragments.

Until fairly recently, breaks were treated mainly with "plaster and time." For the elderly, six months in bed with a broken hip often meant general deterioration, pneumonia, even death. Today, orthopedic surgeons aim to get people out of bed as quickly as possible. To facilitate bone patching, they have pins, screws, plates. A frozen elbow, finger or knee? There are artificial joints. A shattered hip? Install a new ball and socket, very often made of plastic and metal. Does a girl think she is too

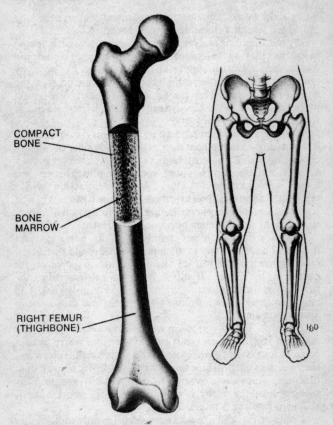

COMPACT
BONE

BONE
MARROW

RIGHT FEMUR
(THIGHBONE)

tall? They can shorten stature by removing up to three inches of me. However, shortening of leg bones is not standard. Too short? Bones can be lengthened, but the procedure is very difficult.

While the orthopedists' work is impressive, the real healing is handled by me. My osteoblasts go into high-speed production, squirting out collagen to be calcified into bone. And I have other interesting repairmen: my osteoclasts. These cells *destroy* bone, trimming off rough edges, helping sculpture the bone back to its original shape.

We bones are prey to a host of strange ailments. In one of the nastiest, aplastic anemia, our marrow simply forgets how to manufacture blood. Excessive radiation or various poisons can bring this on, or it may appear for no known reason. Doctors can only give transfusions and bone-marrow transplants, and pray that we bones will somehow cure ourselves.

Arthritis—inflammation and freezing of our joints—is another problem. Surgery, including replacement of the frozen joint, can be the definitive answer here. In a way bursitis—tennis elbow, glass shoulder, housemaid's knee—might be considered a bone problem, although actually it isn't. Joints have little sacs—bursae—that cushion and lubricate. Occasionally they become inflamed. Several times Joe has had stiff shoulders—this was mild bursitis. We bones get cancer, too. Infection is a worry. Germs hit us via the bloodstream, slip in from wounds in adjacent areas or invade us as the result of a break. Such incursions can lead to the bone inflammation called osteomyelitis—and a very nasty business it can be. Antibiotics are the doctor's first line of defense.

Though I doubt Joe has ever heard of it, one bone ailment that strikes just about everyone to a degree is osteoporosis. When Joe was in his 20s we bones reached our peak density and strength. Then, ever so slowly, our calcium and our other stored minerals started to diminish. We passed them into the blood in greater quantities than we stored them, and the kidneys passed them to the outside. We started to grow less dense, less strong. At first the process was gradual—even at 47 Joe has no symptoms whatever. But later on he will have about one chance in ten of osteoporosis posing difficulties.

For reasons I cannot explain, the process is apt to be far more serious for Jane, his wife. When her ovaries shut down at menopause, the mineral drain is likely to accelerate. By the time she reaches 65, her vertebrae, hips and wrists may become fragile, and a fall that once meant a bruise now may mean a fracture.

Structural and Other Body Components

Osteoporosis remains pretty much of a mystery. About the best advice I can give Joe is this: Accept the fact that we bones are going to grow a little less rugged, and be a bit cautious about jolts and jars.

One final point. Fossil bones have survived tens of millions of years. Bits and pieces of bone from the first men on earth are still turning up. So add that to our credits. In addition to playing key roles in life, we bones come closer to achieving immortality than any other component of Joe's body.

FOOT

JOE IS SOMEWHAT awed by his heart, liver, lungs and other organs. But he tends to regard me as an ungainly, trouble-causing nuisance. I am Joe's left foot. I've been described as everything from an architectural nightmare to an anatomical wonder. The latter, I think, is closer to fact.

Joe has no idea what a complex piece of machinery I really am. There he stands, gazing out a window, his mind pretty much a blank. Yet a great deal is going on inside *me*. In effect, through the intricate interaction of my 26 bones (one fourth of all Joe's bones are in his feet), 107 ligaments and 19 muscles. I am balancing a six-foot, 180-pound pile of flesh and bone. Try balancing *anything* that size on an area no larger than the soles of two feet! It's a tricky business. Messages fly back and forth from the brain. Sensor spots in my soles report that pressure is growing in one area—Joe is tilting slightly. Back come orders: tighten this muscle, relax that one. It would take a good-sized computer to handle a balancing act like that.

Walking is even more complex. My heel takes the initial shock load, which is then transmitted along my five metatarsal

Structural and Other Body Components

bones to the ball of Joe's foot, just behind the toes. Finally, with the big toe, I give a forward thrust. This keeps me quite busy.

But Joe pays more attention to the tires of his car than he does to me. He punishes me unmercifully, then gets annoyed when I hurt. He simply cannot understand it. Let him walk down a sidewalk at a comfortable 100-steps-a-minute pace. That means I'm hitting cement with a 180-pound jolt 50 times each minute, and my partner to the right is doing the same. In his lifetime Joe will walk something like 65,000 miles—which means tens of millions of jolts for me. The wonder is that I don't collapse completely.

For the first million years or so that Joe's ancestors were on earth, things were fine for feet. Everyone walked barefoot (later on, they would wrap feet in animal skins) on yielding, uneven terrain—the finest possible exercise for feet. Then came shoes, cement sidewalks and hard floors. I begin to hurt just thinking about them!

When Joe was a baby, his parents, without knowing it, piled punishment on me. They did not realize that my bones were soft and rubbery (I wouldn't be a finished product until Joe was about 20 years old). They tucked crib sheets tightly enough to produce mild deformities in me and crammed me into shoes and socks, both short enough to do further damage.

Like all young parents, they were anxious for Joe to take his first wobbly steps, and tried to help him. I was still a little bag of pretty soft jelly, not yet ready for walking. It would have been better if they had let Joe decide when he was ready to walk by himself—and left him barefoot until then, or even a month or so afterward.

As a child, Joe got regular checks of heart, lungs and other organs that are rarely defective in the young. But I, a big trouble causer, was ignored. Many doctors figure, I suppose, that sore feet never killed anyone. By the time Joe was four, a podiatrist—foot specialist—would have seen immediately that I needed help. By the time Joe was six, real trouble was under way, as in 40 percent of all kids. My partner and I were going flat, and there were beginnings of toe deformities, caused mainly by heredity and shoes.

Joe got lessons in tooth brushing, hair grooming and ear

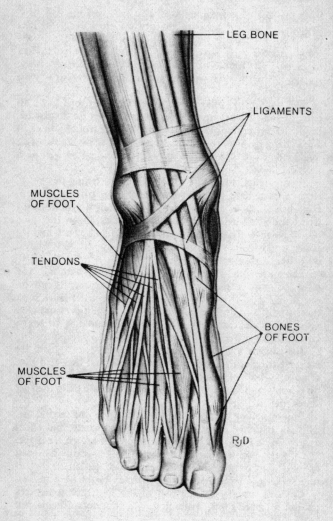

LEG BONE

LIGAMENTS

MUSCLES
OF FOOT

TENDONS

BONES
OF FOOT

MUSCLES
OF FOOT

RjD

191

washing, but no one thought to give him walking lessons—mainly, to walk with toes straight forward. He walked with toes out. Also, his parents bought him shoes that would last—the worst possible thing. Up to age six, Joe should have had his feet measured every four to six weeks and new shoes when necessary. By age 12, he should have been getting new shoes four times a year.

There is an old adage that "when feet hurt, one hurts all over." I can cause symptoms far removed from me: backache, headache, leg cramps and such. Mainly these troubles trace to Joe's changing posture and gait to spare one of my sore spots. I might add that these things have an emotional as well as a physical impact. Sore feet, sour disposition.

By all rights, Joe's wife's foot should be telling this story, since women have four times as much foot trouble as men. High-heeled shoes are to blame. They pitch weight forward where it doesn't belong, shorten calf muscles, throw the spine out of balance. That's why women have so many back and leg pains. And why they kick off shoes at every opportunity. They'd do better to throw them away.

There are some 50 things that can go wrong with me. The most common: corns. When a shoe produces a pressure spot on one of my toes, I respond by piling up protective tissue. Soon there is a pile of dead cells—high enough to put pressure on a nerve below and cause pain. One corn cure would be for Joe to go to bed for a week. Usually, the corns would disappear.

Joe considers himself a quite competent corn surgeon. He isn't. He trims with a razor blade, unsterile, and uses acid corn removers—both of which can lead to infection. What he should do is apply a moleskin plaster to ease immediate pain, then get shoes that fit.

Bunions come when my big toe folds under the second toe. This, in males, is mostly a hereditary deformity, but shoes aggravate it. I respond by building a pad of protective tissue. Usually the problem can be alleviated by a specially designed splint or sling or other mechanical appliance, used in the shoe. If not, surgery to straighten the big toe may be the only answer.

Calluses, usually on the ball of the foot, are sometimes painful pressure spots. Trimming by a foot doctor helps, but wedges, lifts and appliances to produce better balance are the best answer.

Athlete's foot is caused by fungi. These are always present on me, but they cause no harm until they develop and multiply in a moist skin crack or crevice. The best prevention is to keep me dry—not easy, since sweat glands are more numerous on my sole than in any other part of the body except the palms of the hands. If Joe would give me a good wash twice a day, an alcohol rubdown and frequent dustings with powder, the problem would be kept under control. If these things fail, there are always the new antifungus pills.

Everyone has had ingrown toenails. The best treatment is to clean the corners and put a pellet of medicated cotton under the nail. Still a better prevention—trim the nail straight across, and not too short.

Lately, Joe has had a few bouts of coldness and numbness in me—due to poor circulation, a part of the aging process. Get the blood moving faster and the trouble goes away. Tepid baths help to dilate blood vessels and improve circulation. Propping me and my partner up on a desk or hassock also helps. As does a walk.

The very best exercise Joe can give me is walking barefoot, as his ancestors did, over uneven terrain. If he would play golf barefoot, it would be a treat for me. But on hard surfaces I do need shoes for support. And, although Joe will imprison me in these leather cells for two thirds of his life, he still doesn't know how to buy a decent pair. In fact, he spends more time selecting a necktie. Occasionally, when I am giving him a hard time, he may buy a pair of "health" shoes. There is no such thing—any more than there are "health" eyeglasses or "health" dentures. Either a shoe fits or it doesn't.

Joe should buy shoes in the late afternoon, when I've swollen to my largest size of the day. He should insist that the salesman measure *both* me and my partner; often one foot is slightly larger than the other. And the measuring should be done while Joe is standing. (By the way, though I stopped growing when Joe was about 20, I have been elongating and broadening all the years since—Joe was a size 7½ then, but he's a size 8½ now.)

Shoes should be at least half an inch longer than the longest toe. If there isn't room for me to wiggle my toes, Joe should pass up that pair. And forget about "breaking in" shoes. If a shoe isn't comfortable when bought, it's going to cause me—and Joe—trouble. Another thing: too-short socks are almost as bad toe crampers as shoes. Joe should particularly watch those stretch ones.

One final thing: I am threatening Joe here, and he had better pay heed. Ahead lies old age. The great majority of older people have ailing, painful feet from years of misuse. This is one of the main reasons they spend so much time in rocking chairs and on park benches. There they sit, at the very time of life when they are most in need of mild exercise and stimulating activities.

In this sense, I can actually shorten life. If Joe is to avoid this, he had better start giving me the attention—the *serious* attention—I deserve.

HAND

JOE THINKS LOSING eyes or legs would be supreme disasters. Losing my partner and me would be a far greater one. I am Joe's left hand. I can't perform chemical miracles like his liver, or electrochemical wonders like his brain. Basically, I am a piece of machinery, a bewildering array of levers, hinges and power sources, all managed by a master computer—Joe's brain. In complexity I dwarf man-made machines. I am versatile, tireless, swift. If Joe were an exceptional typist, my partner and I could put 120 or more words on paper each minute.

A measure of the importance of any body part is the size of the brain area reserved for its use. We hands have two of the largest spaces in the area of the brain known as the motor cortex. When Joe rotates his thumb, he is witnessing an amazing event. Thousands of messages from the brain are required for the simple act, ordering this muscle to contract, that one to relax; causing this tendon to pull, that one to rest.

From birth to death we hands are almost never still—except for some rest during sleep. During Joe's lifetime I will extend

195

Structural and Other Body Components

and flex finger joints at least 25 *million* times. Legs, arms, shoulders, feet and other parts of his body tire with sustained activity. But how often does he complain about tired hands.

Even when Joe as a baby emerged from the womb we hands were quite well developed. We were strong enough to support his body weight—and before long we would hang from the obstetrician's thumbs. Considering the remoteness of many of the muscles that control me—in Joe's forearm—my strength is surprising. Joe can exert a grip of 90 pounds; if he were superstrong it might go up to 120 or higher. (Women generally have only about half as much grip as a man.)

Like approximately 95 percent of other people, Joe is right-handed. He began to chose handedness when he was about six months old. At the same time he began to coordinate hand and eye movements—learning to look at something and pick it up. This period was a landmark in his development.

Until man's forebears assumed upright posture they were among the most defenseless of creatures: a snack for a lion or a tiger, easy prey for a hyena. But once erect posture freed us hands from the job of locomotion, we could fashion and use weapons and tools. Then the naked ape achieved mastery over the earth and its creatures. Then, too, the jaws, freed of foraging and fighting responsibilities, shrank in size and could begin to experiment with language. As our tasks became more complex, the brain began to grow. Joe, the end product of all this, can give us much of the credit for starting him up the evolutionary ladder.

The strange thing is that meanwhile not a great deal was happening to *us*—we aren't much different structurally from hands of other primates. But we are infinitely more skilled.

We can even substitute for eyes, ears, voice. If Joe were blind, he could use us to read Braille. If deaf, he could "speak" with us by using sign language. Our tactile discrimination is so keen that Joe doesn't have to look at the coins in his pocket to find a quarter. My fingers can pick one out for him. If he were a farmer, he could run soil through his hands and determine its texture; if a housewife, he could judge by feel the quality of a fabric. These are extraordinary achievements.

We hands can take a certain amount of credit for some

important intellectual achievements, too. We played a part in the development of mathematics—the decimal system is based on the ten digits my partner and I possess, as well as Joe's ten toes.

Structurally, we are the most intricate components of Joe's body. In no other part of the body is so much machinery packed into so small a space. I have 8 wrist bones, 5 bones in my palm, 14 in my digits—a total of 27. Add my partner's 27 and we account for more than a fourth of the bones in Joe's body. My supply of nerves to detect heat, touch and pain is one of the most elaborate in the body. I have thousands of nerve endings per square inch, most heavily concentrated in my fingertips. Sensitivity here is extraordinary. Joe can feel his way in the dark, moisten a fingertip and determine direction of the wind and do a thousand other things that he considers commonplace—instead of looking on them as the true wonders they are.

My tendons are the power trains, the connecting linkup between my many jointed bones and the remote muscles which move them. (Joe can feel tendons in his forearm move when he flexes a finger.) For binding material I have a maze of ligaments, plus fascia, which is a layer of connective tissue providing foundation material for nerves, blood vessels and other components. I don't have room for a big network of arteries and veins, but I do have a rich network of capillaries. I suffer on a cold day while the rest of Joe's body is quite comfortable because the peripheral nature of my digits—they are far from Joe's heart—allows his blood to cool.

My digits are, of course, my main working parts. The real virtuoso is my thumb; it is "opposed" to the other four, can swing to touch all of them and provide grip. It does about 45 percent of my useful work—let Joe try to write without it, lift a glass of water or shake hands. Joe could get along quite well without any one of my other four digits, or even if only stubs of them remained. But take away my thumb and I would be like a pair of pliers with one jaw missing. My digits become less independent as they move away from the thumb, and the little fifth one is the least independent of all.

Have I missed any of my other features? Oh yes, fingerprints. These were formed by Joe's fourth month in the womb, and it is

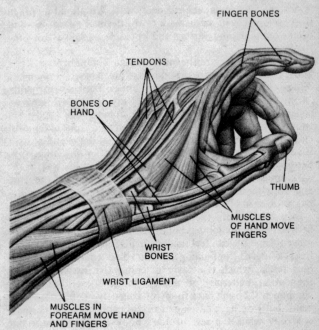

FINGER BONES

TENDONS

BONES OF
HAND

THUMB

MUSCLES
OF HAND MOVE
FINGERS

WRIST
BONES

WRIST LIGAMENT

MUSCLES IN
FOREARM MOVE HAND
AND FINGERS

no news that they are totally individual. No one else on earth has fingerprints exactly like mine. One more thing: my palm contains one of the body's richest supplies of sweat glands. Millions of years ago, when Joe's ancestors were tree dwellers, moist palms gave them a better grip. Now they help him hang onto a baseball bat or steering wheel. Incidentally, Joe's palms (and the soles of his feet) are about the only surfaces of his body that don't tan. They lack the dark pigment melanin—which explains why palms of blacks and whites are much the same color.

Since I play a part in just about everything Joe does, it is little wonder that I am involved in a large number of his accidents. I am burned, mashed, pinched, cut, bruised. I am hit by fungus infections, dermatitis, psoriasis, allergies. My tendons are pulled and torn, my muscles go into spasm. Arthritis and many other diseases attack my joints. Cancer, though, almost never strikes me.

At one point in history, if Joe lost a thumb in an accident, it would have represented calamity. Today, however, a skilled hand surgeon can transfer the index finger, with its nerves, tendons and blood vessels intact, and Joe could have a new thumb. This may sound simple, but it is an operation requiring hours of meticulous work. And, after the surgery, Joe would need months of patient rehabilitation to learn to use his new thumb.

Perhaps the greatest beneficiaries of the new hand surgery are those who come into the world with webbed fingers, extra fingers or some other blunder of nature. Today's skilled hand specialist—part plastic surgeon, part orthopedist, part neurosurgeon, part vascular specialist—can fashion a cosmetically acceptable, satisfactorily workable hand.

Joe is now getting to the age where arthritis takes its worst swipes. This disease can be devastating—swollen, inflamed joints twisting me into bizarre shapes, rendering me virtually useless. Here again, surgeons can sometimes help, by removing thickened and inflamed joint linings, by straightening fingers and restoring the hand to workable shape. If finger joints have been destroyed, they can often install plastic replacements.

Though only subconsciously aware of my importance, people pay unwitting tribute to it in conversation. For instance, they throw hands up in horror, vote thumbs down, ask to be handed something. They win hands down, surrender hands up, warn hands off, equate cold hands with a warm heart. They shake hands in friendship and use the clenched fist for anger. But Joe becomes fully aware of my *real* importance only when something goes wrong—let him burn two of my fingers badly, and he'll find it more disabling than a broken collarbone. Joe should regard me with wonder, as the remarkably sophisticated and indispensable piece of body machinery that I am.

HAIR

FOR ALL PRACTICAL purposes I am useless—one of the few parts of Joe's body with nothing to do. Yet he is more concerned about me than about most of his life-and-death organs. He and Jane, his wife, lavish time, attention and money on me and my associates. I am hair No. 56,789 in Joe's head and will speak for the millions of others scattered over his body.

We hairs come in various sizes and shapes: stiff and short in the eyebrows; long and soft on the head; downy and virtually invisible on most other body areas. There are 100,000 of us on Joe's scalp, 30,000 in his beard. We are among the fastest-growing tissues in his body. Each year Joe will produce about 5½ inches of beard and about 5 inches of scalp hair.

We hairs served primitive man well: brows protected eyes, facial hair gave warmth in winter, pubic and armpit hair lessened chafing. But for the most part these jobs lost importance. Indeed, shaving the beard became a military necessity—the whiskers made too convenient a handle for a foe to hang on to while he went to work with a sword.

200

What are we hairs and where do we come from? Buried about an eighth of an inch down in the corium—the layer of skin beneath the epidermis that contains the blood and nerves—I have a tiny follicle. The follicle is simply a minute hair factory, an amazing and complex affair that operates 24 hours a day for up to seven years and then shuts down for rest and repairs. After a rest period, my follicle will crank up and start producing again. I usually drop out and am replaced by a new hair—Joe loses some 75 of us scalp hairs a day.

At two months our follicles started forming when Joe was in his mother's womb. They began producing a silky down called lanugo. At seven months Joe shed this.

When Joe was a child, soft, short "vellus" hair covered most of his body. At puberty, many of the follicles that had been producing vellus hair changed and started producing the coarser "terminal" hair that Joe has today. Another curious point about hair—eventually many scalp follicles may degenerate and start producing vellus hair instead of terminal hair or they may shut down completely. That's ordinary baldness. A high percentage of men are bald or balding by midlife, but relatively few women.

When Joe reaches old age, we hairs will become smaller in diameter as his factory decreases in size. Our quality, as a general rule, will become poor.

When Joe plucks one of his scalp hairs, he may note a small club at the end. He's afraid the hair won't be replaced. It will. This club is simply the terminal end of a hair from a resting follicle, which is about to be shed anyway.

The essential production of hair follicles is protein. We hairs are made up almost entirely of protein. It's amazing that anything as tiny as a follicle could turn out a product so intricate. My outer layer has overlapping cells that look like shingles on a roof. This layer gives strength and protection. My middle layer contains fatter elongated cells that give bulk. I am quite elastic and under certain conditions can be stretched my length. I am also surprisingly strong and can support about a three-ounce weight.

As my follicle creates and arranges my cells to make this complex structure, it gives me a little squirt of coloring matter, which is parceled out in tiny granules. Hair color depends on the shape, number and distribution of these granules, as well as on the type of pigment present—brown-black or yellow-red. Each follicle also has attached sebaceous glands to provide its hair with lubricating and waterproofing fat.

Newly produced hair cells are living affairs. As they are pushed upward through the hair canal, a hardening process called keratinization sets in. The part of my hair above the surface is dead. The keratin we hairs are made of is also found in the horns of a cow, feathers of a duck and hoofs of a goat.

The production rate of individual follicles varies around Joe's body. Some—like those of his eyebrows and eyelids—rest most of the time. But plucking eyebrows stimulates follicle activity, and results in more speedy regrowth than if they are shaved. My follicle is one of the more active ones. It produces about half an inch of hair a month. The follicles that produce Joe's whiskers are slightly faster. Although Jane has about the same number of follicles as Joe, most of her follicles produce a quite different type of hair. Her body and facial hair is mostly a fine, almost invisible down—the same vellus hair that covered Joe as a child. She can thank her stars that this is so. Otherwise she might be bearded and hairy-chested.

Our follicles produce hair that is straight, wavy or curly. In cross section we might have one of three basic shapes: round, oval or flattened. Round is for straight hair; oval is for wavy hair; flattened is for kinky hair. Of course, there are degrees in between. The flatter we hairs are, the curlier we are; the rounder we are, the straighter.

Joe is now 47 and noticing gray hairs. This is because my pigment glands are slowing production. In time they will shut down entirely. Then Joe will have white hair.

In a sense, we hairs are record keepers for Joe's body. Minute portions of what he consumes are apt to show up in us, particularly metals. Joe frets about lead pollution in today's air from motor exhaust. If he had a snippet of his grandfather's hair, it might contain several times as much lead as Joe's. The old gentleman could have got it from lead plumbing and lead-glazed earthenware. Should someone decide to slip arsenic into Joe's tea, a good chemist could examine his hair and know,

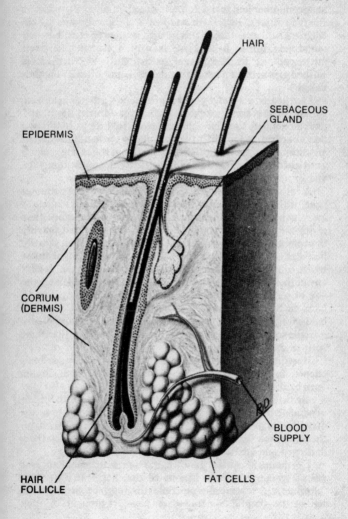

HAIR

SEBACEOUS
GLAND

EPIDERMIS

CORIUM
(DERMIS)

BLOOD
SUPPLY

HAIR
FOLLICLE

FAT CELLS

to within 48 hours, when Joe was dosed.

As a matter of fact, there is talk now of using us hairs to help diagnose disease—adding this to such routine tests as those for blood and urine. A look at us with a scanning electron microscope or by X-ray analysis can show whether Joe is suffering from certain hereditary diseases, and a variety of other things.

Our health is totally dependent on Joe's general health. A variety of diseases involving high fever—scarlet fever and pneumonia among them—can cause our follicles to shut down temporarily and Joe's hair to come out by the handful. And, in an unusual case, sustained strong emotional states might cause an abnormally high number of follicles to enter my resting stage and bring on temporary baldness.

A lot of nonsense has been written about us. One common belief is that we grow after death. Not so. Skin shrinks and falls away, exposing hairs already in existence below the surface, thus giving the *appearance* of growth. Another belief is that shaving thickens and coarsens hair—Jane frets about this when shaving her legs. Again, not so. Still another belief is that baldness traces to poor circulation, too much sun, too little sun. It isn't any of these, and I can prove it. Suppose Joe got a bald patch the size of a saucer. He could have hair grafts containing 8 to 12 hairs each taken from his neck and transplanted to cover the bald spot. And these transplants would thrive on the supposedly infertile soil. So there is far more to ordinary baldness than tight scalp and poor circulation.

Heredity plays a big role. Had Joe's father been bald, Joe's chances for baldness would have been 50-50. Had both parents been bald, his chances would be much greater. Glands also play a role with Joe's hair. At puberty Joe's male glands began producing large amounts of the hormone testosterone. Immediately, terminal hair began sprouting in places previously bare: the pubic area, armpits, and on legs and chest. Downy facial hair darkened and coarsened.

Hormones also affect Jane's hair. During pregnancy she had excess female hormone. She noted that her head hair grew luxuriantly. A few months or so after delivery, she started losing hair by the combful. She fretted and had dark thoughts of going

204

bald. She needn't have worried. In a short time normal hormonal order was restored and her hair problems ended. But if Jane got an overdose of male hormone the result would be disastrous. Normally, Jane's adrenal glands produce only minute amounts of male hormone. But let a tumor stimulate them into overproduction and Jane might well qualify for a job as the bearded lady with a circus.

Thyroid hormone also plays a part. Too much thyroid hormone and hair grows profusely; too little and it is lusterless and tends to fall out.

Like other organs, we hairs have a wide array of diseases to cause us trouble. We can get minute tumors on our follicles which destroy them. We are hit by fungus diseases (ringworm). Certain drugs cause us to fall out—as does excessive vitamin A. Viral and bacterial diseases attack us. One strange ailment is alopecia areata—patchy baldness. Cause? I don't really know. Heredity has something to do with it. But it is the darling of "hair experts." At Joe's age they know that hair is likely to grow back anyway after a few months and that their ministrations will get the credit.

Hair care? A few dos and don'ts cover the essentials. We hairs tend to trap dust, bacteria and other debris, so shampooing once a week or more is a good idea. Too much exposure to summer sun can make hair dry, brittle and discolored; wear a scarf or wide-brimmed hat to protect us. And rinsing or shampooing after swimming in salt or chlorinated water will prevent dryness.

Otherwise, about the best advice I can give Joe and Jane is this: keep your bodies in good health and I will be in good health. When heredity decrees that the time has come for me to take permanent departure from Joe's head, there is little he can do about it. When the time comes for Jane's hair to grow thin and white, she can resort to dye or the wigmaker. But there is little either can do to change our destiny.